Drug Abuse

ISSUES

REFERENCE ONLY

DO NOT REMOVE

Volume 114

Series Editor

Craig Donnellan

Assistant Editor

Lisa Firth

 *Independence*

Educational Publishers
Cambridge

First published by Independence
PO Box 295
Cambridge CB1 3XP
England

British Library Cataloguing in Publication Data
Drug Abuse – (Issues Series)
I. Donnellan, Craig II. Series
362.2'9

ISBN 1 86168 347 2

Printed in Great Britain
MWL Print Group Ltd

Layout by
Lisa Firth

Cover
The illustration on the front cover is by
Angelo Madrid.

CONTENTS

Introduction

Drug Abuse is the one hundred and fourteenth volume in the **Issues** series. The aim of this series is to offer up-to-date information about important issues in our world.

Drug Abuse looks at the problem of drug misuse, the issues involved in young people's drug use and the legal status of different drugs.

The information comes from a wide variety of sources and includes:
Government reports and statistics
Newspaper reports and features
Magazine articles and surveys
Website material
Literature from lobby groups
and charitable organisations.

It is hoped that, as you read about the many aspects of the issues explored in this book, you will critically evaluate the information presented. It is important that you decide whether you are being presented with facts or opinions. Does the writer give a biased or an unbiased report? If an opinion is being expressed, do you agree with the writer?

Drug Abuse offers a useful starting-point for those who need convenient access to information about the many issues involved. However, it is only a starting-point. At the back of the book is a list of organisations which you may want to contact for further information.

*****

About drugs

Drugs and their effects

What is a drug?

A drug is any substance, solid, liquid or gas that brings about physical and/or psychological changes in the body.

The drugs of most concern to the community are those that affect the central nervous system. They act on the brain and can change the way a person thinks, feels or behaves. These are the psychoactive drugs.

Where do drugs come from?

Drugs are derived from a range of sources. Many are found in plants, for example nicotine in tobacco; caffeine in coffee; and cocaine from the coca plant. Morphine and codeine are derived from the opium poppy, while heroin is made from morphine or codeine. Marijuana is the leaf, buds and seed heads of the cannabis plant and hashish and hash oil are the plant's resin.

Alcohol is a product of the natural process of fermentation, which happens when fruit, grain or vegetables decompose. Fungi, such as magic mushrooms, and some types of cactus plants are considered drugs because of their hallucinogenic properties. Medicines are manufactured from both natural and artificial chemicals.

Classifying drugs

The two most common ways of classifying drugs are:
- according to the legal status of the drug; and
- according to the drug's effects on the central nervous system.

Classifying by legal status

Most legal drugs are subject to restrictions and controls that affect their availability, quality and price. Illegal, or illicit, drugs have no quality or price controls. This means that anyone using these drugs can never be sure of the drug's strength or purity. Various batches of an illegally manufactured drug may have different mixtures of the drug and other additives, such as talcum powder, sugar, and caffeine. Sometimes the additives can be poisonous.

Classifying by effects

There are three main types of drugs, classified according to the effect the drug has on the central nervous system: depressants, stimulants and hallucinogens.

There are three main types of drugs: depressants, stimulants and hallucinogens

---

Depressant drugs

Depressant drugs don't necessarily make a person feel depressed. They slow down the functions of the central nervous system.

In small quantities they can cause a person to feel more relaxed and less inhibited. In larger quantities they may cause unconsciousness, vomiting and, in some cases, death.

Depressants affect concentration and coordination. They slow down a person's ability to respond to unexpected situations. Depressant drugs include:
- alcohol, or 'booze', 'grog'
- barbiturates, including Seconal, Tuinal and Amytal
- benzodiazepines (minor tranquillisers), or 'benzos', 'tranx', with brand names such as Rohypnol, Valium, Serepax, Mogadon, Normison and Eupynos
- cannabis, or 'pot', 'mull', 'dope'
- GHB (Gamma-hydroxybutrate), or 'GBH', 'fantasy'
- opiates and opioids, including heroin, or 'H', 'smack', and morphine, codeine, methadone, and pethidine
- some solvents and inhalants, or glue, 'chroming'. Many inhalants are common household products.

Stimulant drugs

Stimulants act on the central nervous system to speed up the messages going to and from the brain. Stimulants can make the user feel more awake, alert or confident. Stimulants increase heart rate, body temperature

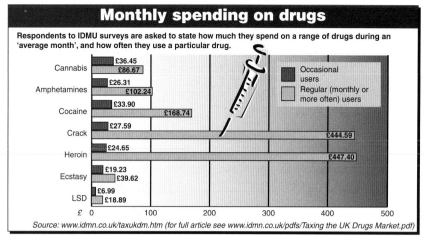

Monthly spending on drugs

Respondents to IDMU surveys are asked to state how much they spend on a range of drugs during an 'average month', and how often they use a particular drug.

Occasional users
Regular (monthly or more often) users

Drug	Occasional	Regular
Cannabis	£36.45	£86.67
Amphetamines	£26.31	£102.24
Cocaine	£33.90	£168.74
Crack	£27.59	£444.59
Heroin	£24.65	£447.40
Ecstasy	£19.23	£39.62
LSD	£6.99	£18.89

£ 0   100   200   300   400   500

Source: www.idmn.co.uk/taxukdm.htm (for full article see www.idmn.co.uk/pdfs/Taxing the UK Drugs Market.pdf)

and blood pressure. Other physical effects include reduced appetite, dilated pupils, talkativeness, agitation, and sleep disturbance.

Overdose occurs when the amount of the drug taken exceeds the body's ability to cope with it

---

Large quantities of stimulants can 'over-stimulate' the user, causing anxiety, panic, seizures, headaches, stomach cramps, aggression and paranoia. Prolonged or sustained use of strong stimulants can also cause these effects. Strong stimulants can mask some of the effects of depressant drugs, such as alcohol, making it difficult for the user to judge exactly what effects the drugs have on them.

Mild stimulants include:

- caffeine in coffee, tea and cola drinks
- ephedrine used in medicines for bronchitis, hay fever and asthma
- nicotine in tobacco is also a stimulant, despite many smokers using it to relax.

Stronger stimulants include:

- amphetamines, including illegal amphetamines, or 'speed', 'crystal meth', 'ice', 'shabu'
- cocaine, or 'coke', 'crack'
- ecstasy, or 'E', 'XTC'
- slimming tablets such as Duromine, Tenuate Dospan and Ponderax.

Hallucinogenic drugs

Hallucinogens affect perception. People who have taken them may see or hear things that aren't really there, or what they see may be distorted in some way. The effects of hallucinogens vary greatly. It is impossible to predict how they will affect a particular person at a particular time.

Other effects of hallucinogenic drugs include dilation of pupils, loss of appetite, increased activity, talking or laughing, a sense of emotional and psychological euphoria and wellbeing, jaw clenching, sweating, panic, paranoia, loss of contact with reality, irrational or bizarre behaviour, stomach cramps and nausea.

Hallucinogens include:

- datura
- ketamine, or 'K', 'Special K'
- LSD (lysergic acid diethylamide), or 'trips', 'acid', 'microdots'
- magic mushrooms (psilocybin), or 'gold tops', 'mushies'
- mescaline (peyote cactus)
- PCP, or 'angel dust'.

Cannabis is a depressant as well as a hallucinogen. Ecstasy can also have hallucinogenic qualities.

What factors determine a drug's effects?

As well as the effect the drug has on the central nervous system (depressant, stimulant, hallucinogen), there are a number of factors that will determine how a particular drug will affect an individual including:

- **How much of the drug is used and how often.** Generally, the more used, the greater the effect. Overdose occurs when the amount of the drug taken exceeds the body's ability to cope with the drug.
- **How the drug is used or administered.** Generally, drugs that are injected or inhaled act very quickly and the effects are more intense. Snorting through the nose is the next fastest-acting method of administration, while the effects of drugs eaten or swallowed take longer to occur.
- **Physical characteristics.** Height, weight and gender also influence drug effects. The proportion of body fat, rate of metabolism, and the stage of the menstrual cycle can all influence the intensity and duration of drug effects.
- **Mood and environment of the user.** How a person is feeling can have a significant impact on drug effects, as can the social setting of drug use. Users are more likely to enjoy the experience in a comfortable social atmosphere than in a threatening environment.
- **Tolerance to the substance.** The first time a person uses a drug, they have a very low tolerance and are likely to feel the effects very strongly. The more often the drug is used, generally the less intense the effects will be. This results in the need to take larger amounts in order to obtain the desired effect.
- **Polydrug use (using more than one drug).** Users often have a primary drug of choice, but will use one or more other drugs to increase or reduce the effects of the primary drug of choice or as a substitute. Combining drugs can increase or alter the usual effects, often in unpredictable ways.

- The above extract is reprinted with kind permission from the Australian Drug Foundation, DrugInfo Clearinghouse http://druginfo.adf.org.au. See page 41 for address details.

© Australian Drug Foundation

Drugs: key facts

	Class	More details	Estimated no. users	Users, % population	Average price	Deaths, 2003**
Cocaine	A	Slang: coke, snow, charlie, C Looks: white powder, often wrapped in small packets of paper or clingfilm Taken: Sniffed up the nose or injected	755,000	2.4	£40 per gram	113
Crack	A	Slang: rock, wash, stone Looks: small cystals of cocaine – the size of raisins Taken: smoked	55,000*	0.2	£15-25 per rock	See note below**
Ecstasy	A	Slang: E, mitsubishis, rolexes Looks: tablets of different colours and shapes Taken: swallowed	614,000	2.0	£2-7 per pill	33
Heroin	A	Slang: H, smack, skag, horse, junk, brown Looks: off-white, browny powder, usually wrapped in small packets of paper Taken: injected, smoked or sniffed through the nose	43,000*	0.1	£40-90 per gram	591
LSD	A	Slang: trips, acid, tabs, micro-dots Looks: very small paper squares with a picture on them Taken: sucked and swallowed	76,000	0.2	£1-5 per tab	-
Mushrooms	A	Slang: mushies, happies, sillies, 'shrooms Looks: brown, dried-up mushrooms Taken: usually eaten, but can be made into a tea-type drink	260,000	0.8	-	-
Amphet-amines	A/B	Slang: speed, uppers, whizz, amph, sulphate Looks: dirty white or orangey yellow powder or tablets Taken: swallowed, smoked or sniffed up the nose, injected, or can be mixed with liquid and drunk	483,000	1.5	£8-15 per gram	33
Cannabis	C	Slang: grass, blow, weed, spliff, ganja, dope, hash Looks: cannabis resin usually looks like small brown lumps. The leaves, stalks and seeds of the cannabis plant look like greeny-brown tobacco Taken: it's made into a 'joint' which looks a bit like a cigar-ette. It can be smoked on its own, in a special pipe or even cooked and eaten	3,364,000	10.8	£40-140 per ounce depending on type and quality	11
Any drug			3,854,000	12.3		2,445**

Figures for heroin and crack may be underestimates as types of groups that use these, e.g. people living in homeless hostels, tend not to overlap with crime survey respondents.
** *Mentioned on death certificate where cause of death is listed as drug poisoning. More than one drug may have been present so, for example, a death involving heroin but where cannabis was also found will show up in both heroin and cannabis figures. Cocaine and crack are indistinguishable in the body after death so are not shown seperately. Total deaths includes anti-depressants and painkillers such as paracetamol.*
- *None or no available data.*

Data for England and Wales. Sources: Usage Estimates - British Crime Survey 2003-04, Crown copyright. Street Price - Drugscope Survey 2005. Deaths: ONS, Crown copyright. More Details: Dept. of Health, 'Drugs: the facts', Crown copyright.

Instant expert

Drugs and alcohol

People have been using substances to lift their spirits for millennia. Techniques for fermenting beer and related tipples are known from Egypt and Sumeria 4,000 years ago, and they soon spread across the inhabited world. Coca leaves (the source of cocaine), tobacco, and caffeine were also popular with ancient cultures.

Humans may even have an evolutionary predisposition to seek out narcotics, even though they can be addictive and damaging. Some people may have genes which make them more genetically prone to drug addiction than others. Even some animals – jaguars, lemurs and bees, for example – have a habit of getting high.

There is an enormous amount of research on drug taking, examining both legal highs, such as alcohol, nicotine and caffeine, and illegal stimulants, such as marijuana, LSD, cocaine, ecstasy, amphetamines,

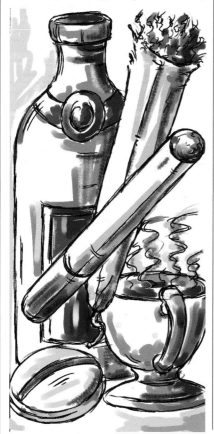

heroin and magic mushrooms and the so-called date-rape drugs rohypnol and GHB.

Alcohol – Some experts believe that the world's first impromptu breweries might have been created when grain stores became drenched with rain and warmed in the sun. Ever since, humans have discovered that alcohol reduces their inhibitions, impairs their judgement, affects sexual desire and performance, creates beer bellies and leads to hangovers (and dubious cures).

Binge drinking is an ever-increasing health concern, and when not consumed in moderation, alcohol can lead to liver problems, brain damage and infertility. Drinking whilst pregnant can also damage the unborn child. It is not all bad news though: studies show that some types of booze, such as red wine, are rich in antioxidant polyphenols which can help prevent heart disease and cancer.

Humans may have an evolutionary predisposition to seek out narcotics

---

Marijuana, once the preserve of hippies, is now regularly smoked by millions of people in the US and UK. Around 14.6 million Americans have used marijuana in the last 30 days. Though still controversial, support for controlled legalisation of this most common illegal drug is growing.

That support is bolstered by research showing that cannabis (and psychoactive extracts such as THC or cannabinoids) can provide relief for sufferers of multiple sclerosis, Alzheimer's disease and epilepsy. Cannabis can also help to improve appetite and decrease weight loss in AIDS victims and may be able to

slow the growth of cancerous tumours.

However, detractors argue that the long-term effects of smoking dope on the brain are unclear, that it decreases fertility, damages the unborn foetus, can contribute to cot death in babies born to dope-smoking parents, and may lead to memory loss, schizophrenia, depression and other illnesses.

Ecstasy, or MDMA, was allegedly first prescribed as an anti-depressant. It was also used by American marriage counsellors and psychotherapists in the 1970s. The drug made patients feel less anxious and more open, accepting and empathic. But notoriety for the drug in the UK did not come until it was popularised by the rave dance scene in fields and warehouses in the late 1980s. Use of the drug is now common in mainstream clubs and 2 million or more British youngsters pop the tablets at weekends. Clubbers enjoy the feelings of emotional closeness, rushes of energy, increased stamina, heightened sense of touch and other effects.

Critics say that regular ecstasy use is a recipe for causing memory loss and lasting damage to the brain's serotonin-producing neurons. Users can die from fatal overheating or a dangerous build-up of water on the brain. Ecstasy causes other problems such as stifling sex drive and damaging babies in the womb.

Tablets contaminated with other compounds are part of the problem and many tests have been developed to check for purity. Controversial research found evidence of a link between ecstasy and Parkinson's disease in 2002, though the finding was later retracted. Other animal studies conversely hinted that ecstasy might actually help treat the symptoms of Parkinson's disease. Some experts point to the fact that despite the drug's massive popularity, ecstasy deaths remain extremely rare: downhill skiing kills more people.

Controversial medical trials are testing the use of MDMA to treat post-traumatic stress disorder in victims of rape and violent crime.

Cocaine comes from the coca plant, the leaves of which have been used by Native South Americans for 3,000 years as a mild stimulant. Cocaine itself was first developed as a local anaesthetic, but has been a popular street drug since the 1970s. Today it is used by millions of people in the US alone and up to 150,000 end up in emergency rooms with heart attacks or other side effects. It acts on the brain's dopamine system, and is thought to mimic the thrill of desire and anticipation.

Cocaine is highly addictive – many users become dependent after a year or two, and some research suggests that just a single dose could get you hooked. Use of the drug is linked to high blood pressure, deadly heart conditions and violent behaviour. Therapies to help addicts conquer their dependence include vaccines and related methods, which use antibodies to bind cocaine and stop it reaching its target in the brain. Other drugs can block cocaine cravings.

Nicotine comes from the leaves of the tobacco plant and was first cultivated and used by Native Americans 8,000 years ago. Early European settlers in the Americas cultivated it as a cash crop for export, and smoking became popular back home in Europe during the 1600s. These days, an estimated 46 million Americans smoke 420 billion cigarettes per year. Smoking was thought to have few ill effects until researchers noticed that lung cancer prevalence rose enormously, along with the popularity of cigarette smoking in the twentieth century.

Today the 40-plus known carcinogenic chemicals in tobacco smoke are linked to cancers including those of the stomach, lung, pancreas, cervix and kidney. Research has also shown that nicotine or other tobacco chemicals can increase the speed of growth of tumours, cause cot death in the children of smokers, kill brain cells and lead to heart disease, strokes, emphysema and even mental illness.

Passive smoking is also widely thought to be a dangerous activity and has been linked to an increase in cancers, heart disease and stroke, as well as lower than average IQ levels in children. Some people may be genetically-prone to nicotine addiction, and teenagers are more likely to become addicted than adults. Scientists are developing a controversial vaccine which could be used to protect young people against cigarette addiction.

Caffeine is found in around 60 known plant species, is a key ingredient of coffee, tea and chocolate, and is the world's most popular stimulant. Tea has been popular in China for at least 3,000 years, but possibly for much longer. Caffeine is used by billions of people to boost alertness.

The drug increases blood pressure and stimulates the heart, lungs and other organs. There have been few verifiable links between caffeine and serious health problems, though research has shown it can increase sensitivity to pain, cause panic attacks and play havoc with sleep cycles. Some role in heart disease and cancer has been suggested, but not proven. Research has hinted that caffeine perhaps offers some unusual benefits by protecting against diabetes and radiation poisoning. Critics argue that addictive caffeine – supposedly a flavouring – is used by soft drink manufacturers to keep punters coming back for more.
John Pickrell

■ Information from *New Scientist*. Please visit their website at www.newscientist.com for more information.

Seven important drug terms

Tolerance
This happens to people when they use drugs over time. It means their bodies have got used to the drug, so they don't feel it has the same effect on them any more. For the drug to give them the feeling they want, people need to take larger and larger amounts. This is very dangerous because the more you take of a drug – the bigger the risks.

Addiction
When a person becomes dependent on a drug and needs it to get by from day to day.

Overdose
This can happen when someone takes so much of a drug that their body can't cope with it. Taking too much of some drugs can make people collapse or even die.

Withdrawal
The bad feeling someone gets when they stop using certain drugs which they've been dependent on for a long time. Heroin and tranquillisers are examples of drugs which can give people these symptoms.

Stimulants
Some drugs such as ecstasy, speed and cocaine affect people by speeding up their bodies and making them feel excited and energetic. Drugs which have this effect are sometimes called 'uppers'.

Depressants
Some drugs like heroin and tranquillisers affect people by slowing their bodies down and making them feel drowsy and relaxed. Drugs which have this effect are sometimes called 'downers'.

Hallucinogens
Some drugs like LSD (acid) and magic mushrooms make people hallucinate – which means seeing or hearing things that are not really there. Sometimes these types of drugs are called 'trips'.

■ Information from the Department of Health.

Trading places

Ketamine on the rise, ecstasy for 50p and 'two in one' bags of heroin and crack: Max Daly takes a look at the results of this year's UK-wide drug price survey

Ketamine, a veterinary anaesthetic with strong hallucinogenic qualities, is now a significant player in the UK drugs market, a survey of 15 UK towns and cities has found.

Druglink Street Prices 2005 found the drug, which first became popular within the gay clubbing scene, has widened its appeal to a larger group of partygoers, edging its way onto the list of major drugs on sale in eight of the 15 areas.

Carried out among 40 frontline drug services in July, the survey provides the most up-to-date information on average UK street drug prices (non-bulk buys). It found that individual ecstasy pills can now be bought for as little as 50p in Portsmouth and 80p in Cardiff – compared to last year's lowest pill price of £1 in Birmingham. The research also highlights a move by dealers towards selling heroin and crack as a combination package.

Trippy

'Ketamine has now established its place alongside the usual dance scene drugs like ecstasy,' said Pete Hurd of Nottingham drug service Compass. 'It's popular in pre-club bars and has a big following in both gay and straight clubs. It is being taken with other dance drugs by middle class people who like to party hard at the weekend and then go back to work in the week.'

Ketamine is currently a legal drug which will, according to the Home Office, be made a class C drug before the end of the year. The drug is being sold for as low as £15 a gram in London and Nottingham. The average UK-wide cost per gram is £30. The drug's growing popularity has raised the price of ecstasy in some areas.

In Birmingham competition from ketamine has triggered a doubling in the price of the average ecstasy pill from between £1 and £2 to between £3 and £6. Neil Venables, from Holistic Innovative Approaches to Health (HIAH), a young people's drug treatment service in Birmingham, says ketamine has replaced ecstasy for some people. 'Ecstasy pills contain less MDMA than they used to and so it is more of just a stimulant than something that alters your state of mind. People aged 18-25 are taking ketamine for a more trippy night out. You can spot them on the dance floor because they're not dancing, they're sitting down in a bit of a vegetative state.' Venables said ketamine was being taken with crystal methamphetamine on the city's gay club scene.

Class A deals

Heroin prices have fluctuated within different towns and cities in the last year. Some, such as Sheffield – home of the cheapest average gram in the country at £25 – Torquay and Portsmouth, have dipped dramatically.

'Sheffield seems to be a distribution centre for South Yorkshire and the nearer you get to the source the cheaper it is,' says Detective Constable Steve Duce, the force's drug strategy coordinator. According to DC Duce, the average £10 bag of heroin bought in the city contains 0.25g of the drug – higher than usual.

In Portsmouth the price of heroin has halved over the last year, from an average of £65-90 a gram to £40 a gram, as a direct result of a charm offensive on the city by a group of dealers. They arrived in May distributing business cards with price lists offering bags containing 0.3 and 0.4 of a gram for £20 instead of the usual £40 outside rehab centres.

In other areas, including Ipswich and Belfast, heroin – being sold at £90 and £100 a gram respectively – has become more expensive. 'The heroin problem in Belfast is smaller than most other cities because paramilitary groups had a zero tolerance attitude to the drug,' says one drugs worker. 'It has also been harder to move the drug around because of checkpoints and heavy policing. Because of all this the price has stayed high – but I think because of political changes here you will see the price start to drop.'

The survey found that buying heroin by the gram was becoming increasingly rare – most street purchases are of 0.6g and £10 bags – which usually contain between 0.1g and 0.2g.

Street drug prices

Druglink spoke to around 40 frontline drug agencies in 15 UK cities (10 listed) to gauge the latest average street prices for 10 drug varieties. Prices in pounds sterling.

City	Herbal cannabis (ounce)*	Resin cannabis (ounce)	Heroin (gram)	Cocaine (gram)	Crack (rock)	Ecstasy (pill)	Amph. (gram)	Ketamine (gram)	LSD (tab)
London	60	50	40	45	7-15	2	9	15-40	2-3
Manchester	100	50	30-40	40	10-15	3.30	5-10	30-40	-
Birmingham	35	35	35-65	40	10	3-6	10	35	-
Glasgow	100	40	70	40	-	5	-	-	5
Belfast	80	50	100	55	30	3	10	25-30	5
Newcastle	100	30	40	35-40	10-20	2-3	2	-	-
Cardiff	80-100	20	40	35-40	20	80p-2	-	40-50	-
Sheffield	70	70	25	30	10	2	8	-	2
Nottingham	40	40	45	50	10	3	10	15-35	2.50
Portsmouth	100	35	40	45	10	50p-2	5	30	-

Standard quality. Where no price is entered, the market for that drug is too small.   Source: Drugscope 2005

Drug workers say heroin and crack are now not just being sold by the same dealer, but in the same bag. The survey found an array of 'all in one', 'two for one', 'party pack', 'free slithers of crack with heroin' and '£5 deals for sex workers' on sale in various parts of the country.

For example, in London, dealers commonly offer bags of brown and white – two £10 bags of heroin and one £10 rock of crack side by side – for £25. Crack is usually sold in blue wraps and heroin in white or striped wraps. Gary Sutton of Release says prices, quality and weights can vary across the capital. 'Some say that you get bigger £10 rocks in north London than in the south. But it is certainly a buyer's market on giro day and a seller's market on Sundays and bank holidays.'

Regional traits

Interestingly, crack is rarely sold in Glasgow and Belfast. Instead users buy powder cocaine and 'wash it up' at home using ammonia-based household cleaning products to create rocks. Craig Sherry, from Glasgow East Community Addiction Team, says:

'Crack is relatively new to Glasgow, we started seeing people using it two years ago. We have very few crack-only addicts here, it's mainly people using as a secondary drug to heroin. They are making rocks themselves because it is cheaper. Scots can be a bit thrifty. They know what they are getting and they have been shown how to wash it up by friends. It's very simple. Scottish drugs users are very DIY orientated.'

Neighbouring cities

Middlesbrough and Newcastle appear from the statistics to have similar priced heroin per gram, at £35 and £40 respectively. Yet this does not represent the true picture. Drug workers say the majority of the heroin sold in Newcastle is first bought in Middlesbrough before being diluted with cheaper chemicals or simply reduced. Most £10 bags bought in Middlesbrough contain 0.2g compared to 0.1g in Newcastle.

Amphetamine has become more popular in the past few months in Newcastle and Nottingham. In Newcastle a gram of speed can be bought for as little as £2 and is more popular as a partner drug among injecting drug users than crack. Valium is popular in Glasgow, London and Birmingham.

The survey also reveals the vast disparity of the price of cannabis, from between £20 and £160, in its various forms. Resin is rarely bought in Nottingham, while Gloucester has the cheapest herbal cannabis.

Cocaine has generally dropped gently in price in most towns and cities, with the average UK cost of a gram down from around £50 to £40. The cheapest cocaine, £25 a gram in Middlesbrough, is, according to drug workers, chiefly made up of bi-carbonate of soda.

■ Information from DrugScope. Visit www.drugscope.org.uk for more information or see page 41 for details.
© DrugScope

Ketamine

Ketamine is a short-acting but powerful general anaesthetic which has been used for operating on humans and animals. It has powerful hallucinogenic qualities. Ketamine first appeared on the streets in the States in the 70s.

ID: Green, K, special K, super K, vitamin k

Appearance and use: Legally produced ketamine comes in liquid form which is injected. The illegally produced version usually comes as a grainy white powder which is snorted or bought as a tablet.

Purity: Legally produced ketamine will be pure. But illegally produced tablets are commonly found with ephedrine added. Sometimes these are passed off as ecstasy.

The effects:
■ Ketamine can cause perceptual changes like LSD, in addition to its effects on reducing bodily sensation. Users can trip for up to an hour and may feel after-effects for some hours.
■ It can give the user an 'out of body' experience.
■ Some users say it feels like their mind and body have been separated.
■ In some cases, users may be physically incapable of moving while under the influence.

Chances of getting hooked: You can become psychologically but not physically dependent on ketamine.

The risks:
■ Because you don't feel any pain when you're on ketamine, you're in danger of injuring yourself badly and having no idea you've done it.
■ High doses, especially with other depressant drugs like alcohol, can dangerously supress breathing and heart function.
■ Ketamine is very dangerous when it is mixed with other drugs or even alcohol, for example it can lead to unconsciousness with depressant drugs or alcohol. It can also cause high blood pressure, which can be particularly dangerous with drugs like ecstasy or amphetamines.
■ It can cause panic attacks, depression and in large doses can exaggerate pre-existing mental health problems such as schizophrenia.
■ If high enough doses are taken, the anaesthetic effect can result in death from inhaling vomit.

The law: Ketamine is a prescription only medicine. You could be prosecuted for supplying it and that includes giving it to friends.

Fact: Passing drugs among friends is supplying in the eyes of the law.

Fact: A drug conviction could stand between you and your ideal job.

■ The above information is reprinted with kind permission from FRANK. Visit www.talktofrank.com for more information or see page 41 for details.
© Crown copyright

Ecstasy could harm memory

Information from the Society for the Study of Addiction

Heavy ecstasy users are at risk of long-term mental impairment, according to a new study published today (1 September 2005) in the international journal *Addiction* (101/9).

The researchers found that nearly half of current users and over half of former users in their study sample met the clinical criteria for substance-induced cognitive disorder, such as memory impairment. Indeed, cognitive disorder was present in some subjects five months after they had stopped using ecstasy.

The research group, from the University Hospital of Hamburg-Eppendorf, Germany, investigated four groups of 30 people matched as closely as possible for age, gender and education level. The groups consisted of current users, former users, people who used a range of drugs not including ecstasy (polydrug users), and drug-naïve controls. Ecstasy users very often use a range of other substances alongside ecstasy, hence the need to match them against the polydrug group.

Previous research has relied on participants' self-report of their symptoms, but in this study the subjects' mental condition was assessed by trained psychologists according to standard clinical diagnostic criteria. Interestingly, the four groups did not differ markedly from each other, or from the general population, in the prevalence of mental disorders unrelated to substance use. However, the ecstasy users, many of whom were defined as heavy users, suffered from a wide range of substance-induced cognitive, mood and anxiety disorders. Furthermore, 73% of them were diagnosed as having been clinically dependent on ecstasy at some point in their lives.

1 September 2005

■ The above information is reprinted with kind permission from the Society for the Study of Addiction's *Addiction* Journal website. For more information please visit the following website: www.addictionjournal.org

---

Ecstasy

How it works

Its medical name is 3,4 methylene-dioxymethamphetamine or MDMA and it comes in tablets with pictures stamped on it. MDMA tells your brain to flood itself with massive amounts of serotonin, the natural chemical which keeps you happy. Then your tanks are empty and you feel grotty for a week while your brain makes some more. Scientists know that large amounts damage your brain's serotonin system permanently.

E is made in a lab but the process of making it can easily go wrong, and can produce some other nasty chemicals which severely damage your brain. Much of what is sold as E contains a tiny amount of the stuff cut with God knows what. Aspirin, sleeping pills, speed, dog worming pills and a lot else besides have been flogged as really good stuff.

What the law says

The law takes E very seriously – it's a Class A drug like heroin or cocaine. This can mean that you can get a very heavy fine or up to 7 years for possessing it and up to life in prison for supplying it – which includes giving it to anyone as well as selling it.

History factoid

It was discovered in 1912 by a German chemist but didn't get popular till the 1980s and the invention of disco – which turned into house music – which turned into today's garage, techno, drum'n'bass etc.

Amazing thing about it

Many recent top club tunes were programmed to sound better on E.

■ The above information is reprinted with kind permission from Doctor Ann. Visit www.doctorann.org for more information or see page 41.

The cocaine explosion

Middle classes are blamed for soaring levels of abuse

An explosion in cocaine use among the middle classes is fuelling soaring levels of hard drug abuse.

The number of cocaine users has doubled since Labour launched its high-profile war on drugs in 1998, and almost trebled over the past decade, Government figures revealed yesterday (26 May 2005).

Anti-drugs campaigners have blamed the disturbing trend on plummeting street prices creating a mass market.

A line of cocaine now costs £2.50 in some areas – less than a glass of wine – bringing what was once an expensive drug within reach of the middle classes.

Latest Home Office figures reveal the existence of around 1.23 million Class A drug users in Britain

Almost 9 per cent of under-25s now admit having taken the drug, including 5 per cent who have done so within the last year.

With use of ecstasy and heroin also on the rise, latest Home Office figures reveal the existence of around 1.23 million Class A drug users in Britain, not including the under-16s.

This is an increase of a third since Labour came to power and includes a growing army of around 850,000 who have taken cocaine in the past year.

International research reveals that Britain has the worst record on drug abuse in the EU. Yesterday opposition critics accused the Government of failing to get to grips with the hard drug epidemic, while campaign groups demanded a fundamental rethink of efforts to educate the young.

By Matthew Hickley, Home Affairs Correspondent

'Previously cocaine was very much the preserve of people with lots of money, such as rock stars,' said a spokesman for the DrugScope campaign. 'Now a lot of young professionals are using it recreationally.

'We need to work harder to get the message across that cocaine is a dangerous drug.'

Seven years ago Tony Blair unveiled ambitious targets to cut hard drug abuse by this year, particularly among youngsters. Since then the figures have got worse and the targets were quietly dropped.

The Government has instead focused its main efforts on the under-25s to try to wean the next generation off hard drugs.

But the figures from the British Crime Survey show the proportion of that age group admitting using cocaine soared by 55 per cent between 1998 and 2004.

Use of dangerously addictive crack cocaine rose by 36 per cent.

Among the 16 to 50 age group, cocaine use rose 97 per cent after the Government launched its drugs strategy in 1998.

While the total number of drug users has remained roughly stable since 1998, the balance has shifted towards the most dangerous drugs – cocaine, crack and heroin.

Shadow Home Secretary David Davis said: 'The Government haven't lost the war on drugs. In fact, they haven't even begun to fight it.'

David Raynes of the National Drug Prevention Alliance added: 'The Government's whole strategy is not succeeding. Downgrading cannabis sent a mixed message.

'Schools are teaching youngsters the facts about drugs, but not how to resist peer pressure to take them.'

Home Office Minister Paul Goggins claimed the Government had made 'significant progress', with more drugs seized and more users in treatment.

He said the new Drugs Act would give police and the courts tougher powers to lock up dealers and direct addicts into treatment.

■ This article first appeared in the *Daily Mail*, 27 May 2005.

Tackling crack misuse

Government and treatment services failing to tackle crack misuse

The Government and drug treatment agencies must do more to stem the UK's growing crack misuse problem, according to a new report out today (26 July 2005) from social care charity Turning Point. The report finds that while more people now report using crack than heroin, treatment services are still heavily focused on heroin use, with primary heroin users accounting for 78 per cent of those in treatment.

More worryingly, there is a particularly chaotic group of people who use both crack and heroin heavily, who face severe health and social problems and are responsible for a disproportionate level of drug-related crime.

The Crack Report, out today, finds that:

- Crack use is rising with 79,000 people admitting to using the drug in the last year compared to 63,000 in previous years. This means that more people now admit to using crack than to using heroin (64,000).
- Treatment services are not meeting the needs of crack users. In research with drug users in treatment, 78 per cent were heroin users and just 7 per cent were using crack. The most chaotic group, using both drugs, accounted for 15 per cent of those in treatment and experience particular health and social problems.
- Substantial quantities of crack are entering the UK and the amount appears to be rising. The number of crack seizures rose by 15 per cent in 2001/02 while seizures of heroin fell by 16 per cent in the same period.
- Action needs to be taken to ensure effective treatment services for people using crack within the community and the criminal justice system – the number of known crack offenders has risen by 326 per cent since 1997.

Lord Victor Adebowale, Chief Executive of Turning Point, said: 'While not the epidemic that many people feared, crack misuse is a steadily growing social problem. It is transforming the UK drug markets and our response to tackling it needs to equally transform. Crack misuse is implicated in a range of social problems – it is interwoven with prostitution and dramatically undermines regeneration and neighbourhood renewal initiatives. The Government has taken significant steps but it is not moving quickly enough and neither are treatment agencies.

'Without urgent action, we face an escalation of the crack problem and a continued growth in the number of crack users in future generations.'

The report calls for government and treatment agencies to take rapid action to tackle the problems associated with crack misuse, specifically:

- All treatment services need to be able to meet the needs of crack users. The National Treatment Agency, responsible for overseeing drug treatment services, should produce guidelines setting out exactly what is expected.
- There should be a training programme for drug treatment workers and related staff such as the police, probation officers, youth offending teams ensuring they are able to deal with crack misuse.
- There should be further investment in crack-specific services, including residential services.

Turning Point and COCA (Conference on Crack and Cocaine) have worked together to produce guidelines for all treatment services to help them ensure they are fully meeting the needs of service users. These will be distributed to treatment agencies and professionals.

26 July 2005

- Information from DrugScope. Visit www.drugscope.org.uk for more information or see page 41 for details.

© *DrugScope*

Cocaine/crack

How it works

Cocaine occurs naturally in the leaves of the South American coca plant, although it's usually treated before it hits the streets. It comes as a white powder – cocaine hydrochloride – though people still chew the original coca leaves sometimes. Most coke users sniff it up their noses using a rolled-up piece of paper, or banknote to show off. Scientists think it works by overdosing your nerves on a natural brain messenger that tells them to feel pleasure, called dopamine. However, cocaine stops you making dopamine after you sniff it for a while, so you can't feel happy again until you get more cocaine. Then you get addicted just to feel normal.

Crack is a derivative of cocaine which comes in small white crystals. When heated they make a 'crack' or 'popping' sound. Crack smoke rushes to your brain and you get a mere 2 minutes' intensive rush, followed by a 20 minutes' buzz and then a totally massive crash. It is very, very addictive.

What the law says

It's very illegal – a serious Class A drug, which means that you can get up to 7 years in prison and huge fines for possessing it, and life imprisonment for supplying it.

© *Teenage Health Websites Ltd*

Revealed: how drugs war failed

Low seizure rates give traffickers vast profits from £4bn-a-year business, says report ministers refuse to publish

The profit margins for major traffickers of heroin into Britain are so high they outstrip luxury goods companies such as Louis Vuitton and Gucci, according to a study that Downing Street is refusing to publish under freedom of information legislation.

Only the first half of the strategy unit study led by the former director general of the BBC, Lord Birt, was released last Friday (1 July 2005). The other half was withheld but has been leaked to the *Guardian*.

It says that the traffickers enjoy such high profits that seizure rates of 60-80% are needed to have any serious impact on the flow of drugs into Britain but nothing greater than 20% has been achieved.

The study concludes that the estimated UK annual supply of heroin and cocaine could be transported into the country in five standard-sized shipping containers but has a value which at a conservative estimate tops £4bn.

The report was presented in its full form to Tony Blair in June 2003.

Alan Travis,
Home Affairs Editor

Only 52 of its 105 pages were published on Friday night on the eve of the Live 8 concert, with a note saying the rest was being withheld under the Freedom of Information Act.

The government yesterday defended its decision not to publish the half of the report that delivers a scathing verdict on efforts to disrupt the drugs supply chain. The first 50 pages deal with drug consumption patterns and drug-related crime.

A Downing Street spokeswoman said the second half contained information supplied by law enforcement agencies dealing with security matters, it concerned the formulation of government policy and its publication would be prejudicial to the conduct of public affairs. But critics last night said much of the unpublished material was already in the public domain.

Among the data suppressed because it was supplied by an agency involved in security is a table on page 12 of the report from the National Criminal Intelligence Service showing average street prices for various drugs. It estimates the average cost for a heavy user at £89 a week for cannabis and £525 for crack cocaine – information that is presumably at the fingertips of every hardcore drug abuser and dealer in the country.

Opposition politicians last night criticised the partial suppression of the Birt report on drugs, saying it was a stark example of the misuse of the Freedom of Information Act.

Seizure rates of 60-80% are needed to have any serious impact on the flow of drugs into Britain but nothing greater than 20% has been achieved

The Liberal Democrats' home affairs spokesman, Mark Oaten, called on the information commissioner to order full disclosure. 'What this report shows and what the government is too paranoid to admit is that the "war on drugs" is a disaster. We need an evidence-led debate about the way forward but if they withhold the evidence we can't have the debate.'

Danny Kushlik of the Transform drugs policy foundation, which campaigns for legalisation, said the government was using the act to hide the parts of the report which demonstrated that, far from reducing production, trafficking and supply, prohibition spawned the business.

'The fact that part of the report was released late on Friday night, right before Live 8 and the G8 meeting, shows how intent the government is on "burying bad news". Fortunately, they won't get away with it.'

The suppressed pages say that the drugs supply market into Britain is sophisticated and attempts to intervene have not resulted in sustainable disruption to the market at any level. 'Government interventions against the drug business are a cost of business, rather than a substantive threat to the industry's viability,' it concludes.

An economic model made for Downing Street shows that the profits per kilo for a major Afghan trafficker into Britain carry a profit margin as high as 58% – higher than Louis Vuitton's margin of 48% or Gucci's 30%.

'Because upstream UK suppliers enjoy high profits, they are more able to absorb the cost of interception. Thus upstream seizures may temporarily impact street availability but are unlikely to threaten the viability of any individual business.'

Emphasising the inadequacy of seizure rates, the study says the result over the past 10 to 15 years has been that, 'despite interventions at every point in the supply chain, cocaine and heroin consumption has been rising, prices falling and drugs have continued to reach users'.

It concludes that even if the government succeeded in reducing the availability of drugs, that could backfire because the most addicted, 'high harm' users might commit more crimes to fund the purchase of ever more expensive drugs.

The report says the annual cost of crimes committed by an estimated 280,000 high harm drug users to support their cocaine and heroin habits has reached £16bn a year – a figure which rises to £24bn if the costs to the nation's health and 'social functioning harms' are included.

Only 20% of the 280,000 high harm drug users are receiving treatment or in prison at any one time. The report notes that those who are in treatment tend not to stay with it for long.

It says that more than 3 million people in the UK use illicit drugs every year and compares the 749 deaths annually from heroin and methadone with the 6,000 deaths from alcohol abuse and 100,000 from tobacco. It reveals that there are 674 hospital admissions on mental health grounds resulting from cannabis use, compared to 3,480 for heroin users.

The report says the drug supply business is large, highly flexible and very adaptable, and even if supply-side interventions were more effective it is not clear that the impact of the harm caused by serious drug users would be reduced.

It argues that targeting distributors and wholesalers does remove drugs before they hit the streets in small quantities but such operations are resource-intensive.

Equally, targeting street dealers helps reduce the social problems they cause but dealers are quickly replaced and only tiny quantities of drugs are removed from circulation.

The outlook for stopping drug production in developing countries is equally gloomy and embarrassing to the British government, which is leading attempts to curb heroin production in Afghanistan.

The report says a policy of compensated, forced eradication is very expensive and actually encourages further planting by farmers, while the alternative of a comprehensive set of development interventions is also expensive, takes time and might only displace cultivation to other countries.

The report was supposed to be phase one of Downing Street's reappraisal of official drugs policy.

In December 2003, phase two, titled 'Diagnoses and Recommendations' and which also remains unpublished, was produced by Lord Birt. It ignored the reported ineffectiveness of the attempts to curb drug trafficking and recommended the compulsory treatment of arrested drug addicts. Powers to enable that are contained in the latest drugs legislation.

5 July 2005

© Guardian Newspapers Limited 2005

Understanding the issues

Summary of the Strategy Unit Drugs Project report's main findings

- All drugs have an adverse impact; but heroin and crack are by far the most addictive, expensive and harmful drugs.
- Heroin and/or crack users cause harm to the health and social functioning of users and society as a whole, but users also commit substantial amounts of crime to fund their drug use (costing £16bn a year). Including health and social functioning harms, the harms arising from drug use amount to £24bn a year.
- There are an estimated 280,000 heroin and/or crack users: at any one time, only 20% of high harm causing users are receiving treatment, whilst 80% are not.
- Over the course of a year, two-thirds of high harm causing users engage with either treatment or criminal justice, but:
  → those engaging with treatment tend not to stay with it for long
  → many of those engaging with criminal justice are not formally identified as users or do not have their use dealt with
  → a third of high harm causing users do not engage with either treatment or the criminal justice system.
- The drugs supply business is large, highly flexible and very adaptable; over time the industry has seen consumption grow and prices reduce.
- Interventions at every stage of the production, trafficking, wholesaling and dealing process have resulted overall in modest seizure rates of up to ~20% of total production.
- Even if supply-side interventions were more effective, it is not clear that the impact on the harms caused by serious drug users would be reduced.

© Crown copyright

Drug related deaths down for the third year running

Information from the Department of Health

Figures published today (24 february 2005) by the Office for National Statistics for 1999 to 2003 show that drug-related deaths fell for the third year in a row to reach their lowest level since 1997. The total reduction since 1999 has been 12% and in young people under the age of 20, deaths from drug misuse fell by almost a third from 2002 to 2003.

Public Health Minister Melanie Johnson welcomed today's figures:

'Deaths from drug misuse represent a significant loss of young lives. Many are under 30 and many of these deaths can be avoided. These new figures showing that fewer people have been dying from drug misuse are encouraging and illustrate that the measures put in place to deliver the Action Plan on Drug Related Deaths are helping to save lives.

'Since the Action Plan was published in 2001, our efforts have been focused on improving the surveillance and monitoring of drug use and improving the access to prescribing treatment for those with drug problems. Accessible inform-

ation and support is available to young people and their families on the risks associated with drug misuse through the innovative Frank campaign. We are also getting more people into drug treatment than ever before and this will be boosted by the increase of 55% more funding for Drug Action Teams which will help take forward the positive progress we are already making.

'Although the figures do show significant improvements in tackling the incidence of drug-related deaths, I recognise that there is no room for complacency. We are determined to ensure that more people receive better quality treatment faster than ever before. We will continue to reduce the damage caused by the most dangerous drugs by ensuring that effective treatment is available as soon as it is needed.'

The report breaks down the information to give death rates for individual substances and groups to reveal that in 2003:

- Deaths linked to methadone fell to their lowest level since 1993.
- Deaths linked to heroin or morphine decreased to reach their lowest level since 1997.

In young people under the age of 20, deaths from drug misuse fell by almost a third from 2002 to 2003

- Deaths linked to cocaine or amphetamines fell by over 10% in comparison with the previous year.

24 February 2005

■ The above information is reprinted with kind permission from the Department of Health. Visit www.dh.gov.uk for more information.

© Crown copyright

Drug user numbers set to treble

Health and criminal justice systems may buckle under strain, warns report

The number of hardcore heroin and crack cocaine addicts in the UK could treble in the next 20 years, putting an overwhelming burden on the nation's health and criminal justice systems, according to a government think-tank report.

If current trends continue the numbers addicted to class A drugs could reach the one million mark by 2025, with the associated economic and social costs soaring to more than £35bn.

The report from the science think tank, Foresight, comes amid growing concerns about the handling of the drugs problem in Britain.

There has been more than a threefold rise in the number of known crack offenders in the past eight years. The prevalence of crack cocaine, manufactured from cocaine from South America, is making it harder for psychiatrists to treat patients who often become violent and paranoid.

Drugs charities warned last week that much more needs to be done to help crack users get into early treatment instead of being sent to psychiatric units and then back into the community without help. Most addiction centres focus on treating alcohol and heroin addiction.

> *If current trends continue the numbers addicted to class A drugs could reach the one million mark by 2025*

Institutions already struggling to cope with the impact of illegal drug use could simply buckle under the strain of a threefold increase, according to the Foresight report. It suggests such an increase would place considerable pressure on the government to allow doctors to prescribe heroin and cocaine widely as a crime-reduction measure.

Earlier this month a leaked government document delivered a scathing verdict on efforts to disrupt the drugs supply chain. Profit margins for major traffickers of heroin are so high that seizure rates of between 60 and 80 per cent are needed to have any impact on the flow of drugs into the country, it warned. At present nothing greater than 20 per cent has been achieved.

The Foresight report, prepared by a team of independent researchers led by Professor Neil McKeganey from Glasgow University, warns that the impact on society would be way beyond anything seen to date.

Although some experts have questioned the size of the predicted increase, McKeganey pointed to the growth in drug use in rural areas, increases in the number of women addicts and the reduction in age at which children are starting to use drugs.

'We are facing the possibility that the drug problem within our society could undermine the very fabric of family and public life,' he said. 'We need to start debating this now because there is a real possibility that our police service and health service are going to be completely overwhelmed.'

Other research published last week found that ex-prisoners run a significant risk of death in the two weeks after they are released from jail because they lose their tolerance to heroin while inside jail. The National Addiction Centre, part of the Institute of Psychiatry in London, found they are 40 times more likely to die than the average person during that timespan because of the risk of a drugs overdose.

According to a report by the drugs charity Turning Point, 79,000 people admitted to using crack in the past year. This means that more people now admit to using crack than to using heroin, which stands at 64,000.

Lorna Martin, Jamie Doward and Jo Revill

■ This article first appeared in the *Observer*, 31 July 2005.

World drug use

Statistics taken from the United Nations' Office on Drugs and Crime (UNODC) *2005 World Drug Report*

Size of the global illicit drug market in 2003 by substances

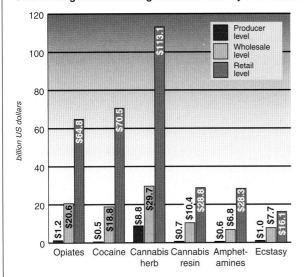

billion US dollars

Legend:
- Producer level
- Wholesale level
- Retail level

Substance	Producer	Wholesale	Retail
Opiates	$1.2	$20.6	$64.8
Cocaine	$0.5	$18.8	$70.5
Cannabis herb	$8.8	$29.7	$113.1
Cannabis resin	$0.7	$10.4	$28.8
Amphetamines	$0.6	$6.8	$28.3
Ecstasy	$1.0	$7.7	$16.1

Extent of drug use (annual prevalence*) estimates 2003/04 (or latest year available)

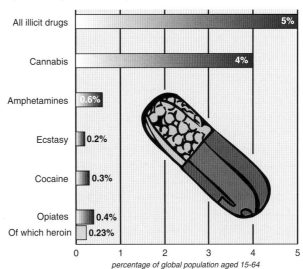

	percentage
All illicit drugs	5%
Cannabis	4%
Amphetamines	0.6%
Ecstasy	0.2%
Cocaine	0.3%
Opiates	0.4%
Of which heroin	0.23%

percentage of global population aged 15-64

* Annual prevalence is a measure of the number/percentage of people who have consumed an illicit drug at least once in the preceding 12-month period.

Sources: UNODC, Annual Reports Questionnaire data, National Reports, UNODC estimates.

Value of illicit drugs at wholesale level (in billion US$) compared to the export values of selected agricultural commodities in 2003

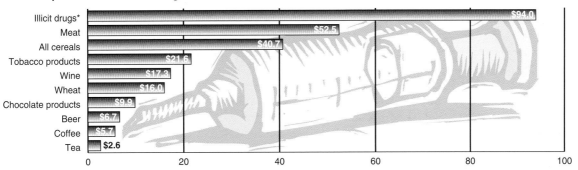

Illicit drugs*	$94.0
Meat	$52.5
All cereals	$40.7
Tobacco products	$21.6
Wine	$17.3
Wheat	$16.0
Chocolate products	$9.9
Beer	$6.7
Coffee	$5.7
Tea	$2.6

* Illicit drugs measured at the wholesale level, used as a proxy for the export price.

Main problem drugs (as reflected in treatment demand) in 2003 (or latest year available)

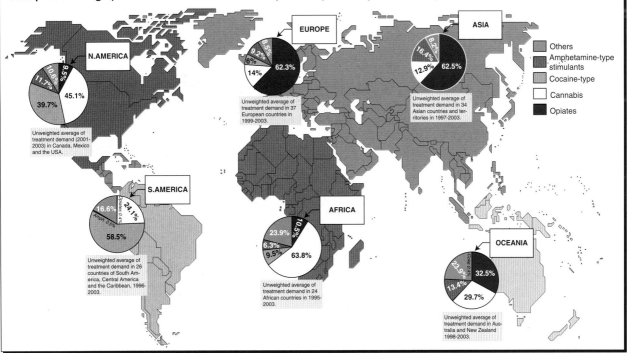

Legend:
- Others
- Amphetamine-type stimulants
- Cocaine-type
- Cannabis
- Opiates

N.AMERICA — 45.1%, 39.7%, 11.7%, 2.9%, 0.6%
Unweighted average of treatment demand (2001-2003) in Canada, Mexico and the USA.

EUROPE — 62.3%, 14%, 6%, 9.2%, 8.5%
Unweighted average of treatment demand in 37 European countries in 1999-2003.

ASIA — 62.5%, 12.9%, 16.4%, 8.2%
Unweighted average of treatment demand in 34 Asian countries and territories in 1997-2003.

S.AMERICA — 58.5%, 24.1%, 16.6%, Opiates 0.4%, Amph. 0.5%
Unweighted average of treatment demand in 26 countries of South America, Central America and the Caribbean, 1996-2003.

AFRICA — 63.8%, 23.9%, 9.5%, 6.3%, 10.5%
Unweighted average of treatment demand in 24 African countries in 1995-2003.

OCEANIA — 32.5%, 29.7%, 13.4%, 23.9%, 0.5%
Unweighted average of treatment demand in Australia and New Zealand 1998-2003.

It's all in the mix

Information from FRANK

If only illegal drugs came in packets with instructions on the outside. We'd all know exactly what the drug would do, how much is too much and what other drugs are to be avoided at the same time.

Unfortunately they don't. And while it's relatively easy to find out about the various effects of illegal drugs it's less easy to find out about safe amounts or dangerous combinations.

Mixing drugs isn't a good idea. It makes the effects unpredictable and the risks harder to define. But if you're hellbent on doing it knowing what's downright stupid before you start could save your life.

In this article, FRANK investigates the drugs that don't mix well with each other.

Cocaine and . . .

Heroin
Known as a speedball. Taken together the drugs double the strength of each other. The coke speeds up your heart straight away, but as it wears off the heroin kicks in and slows down your heart. The result – your heart doesn't know what to do and can lose its rhythm entirely. John Belushi and River Phoenix both died taking speedballs.

Tranquillisers e.g. Temazepam, Valium, Rohypnol
Similar problem. Cocaine is a stimulant and gets your heart racing. Tranquillisers are depressants, they slow down your system. Taking both at the same time confuses the heart and increases the risk of overdose.

FRANK

0800 77 66 00   talktofrank.com
Friendly, confidential drugs advice

LSD
No point at all.
Ecstasy
Doubles the stimulation and puts extra physical strain on your body. Take extra care.

Mixing drugs makes the effects unpredictable and the risks harder to define

---

Alcohol
Drinking alcohol makes the effects of cocaine more powerful (and more dangerous). This combination is common in cocaine-related deaths. Some people set themselves the rule of only one alcoholic drink per line.

Heroin and . . .

Anything
Heroin's the cherry liqueur of the drug world. It's a bad mixer. Taking heroin with anything that makes you sleepy, INCLUDING ALCOHOL, increases your chances of going to sleep and not waking up. And when you're sleepy there's more chance you'll choke on your own vomit. Don't ever take it with GHB.

Same goes for tranquillisers like Valium, Rohypnol, benzos and barbs.
Ecstasy
The effects of ecstasy can mask the effects of the heroin making it easier to overdose on the heroin.
LSD
Psychedelic drugs mess with the effects of heroin making the experience unpredictable and usually unpleasant.

Viagra and . . .

Poppers
Don't mix them. They're both stimulants and taken together can cause a sudden drop in blood pressure that could give you a stroke or a heart attack. Pfizer Inc., the company that manufactures Viagra, has issued a warning about taking the drug with nitrates like poppers.

Ecstasy and . . .

Alcohol
If you've been drinking alcohol it will take longer for you to come up on a pill.

Heavy drinking will dehydrate you and increase your risk of overheating. It places a greater strain on your kidneys and can give you a much worse comedown. If you take ecstasy, stay off the alcohol and try and sip up to a pint of water or fruit juice every hour.
Speed
May make you want to dance like a maniac even more, but it places greater strain on your heart and kidneys and can lead to anxiety, paranoia and burn-out.
Anti-depressants
There are certain kinds of anti-depressants that are really dangerous if taken with E. If you're worried, talk to FRANK.
Nasal decongestants e.g. Sudafed Non-drowsy
Some over-the-counter cold and flu remedies contain Pseudo Ephedrine. Taken with E it can give you heart palpitations and make you feel dizzy and faint.
Cannabis
Mellows out the E and makes it more psychedelic.
LSD
Sometimes called Candyflipping. Reduces the likelihood of a bad trip. But you're less likely to spot the warning signs for ecstasy if you're tripping your head off.

HIV drugs
If you are thinking of taking recreational drugs and you're on HIV medication talk to FRANK. Ecstasy, speed or ketamine taken with drugs like Ritonavir can be deadly.

John Belushi and River Phoenix both died taking speedballs

GHB

Can be fatal when mixed with alcohol and other drugs.

Ketamine and . . .

Anything

Ketamine's an anaesthetic which makes it a depressant. Mixing it with anything else that slows down your body like heroin, tranquillisers or alcohol can be very dangerous. There's a risk you'll feel sleepy and unable to wake, and it's more likely that if you're sick you won't wake up or cough, so you'll choke on your own vomit.

Ecstasy

Some people like to take a bit of ketamine towards the end of their E experience. It can bring back E sensations and feel quite trippy. But it could also leave you with no control over your legs.

Tobacco

Don't, if the ketamine knocks you out you could burn the house down.

Speed and . . .

Tranquillisers/alcohol

Speed overdose is more likely when it's mixed with depressants like alcohol, tranquilisers or heroin.

■ The above information is reprinted with kind permission from FRANK. Visit www.talktofrank.com for more information or see page 41.

© Crown copyright

Dealing with addiction

Information from KidsHealth

Jason and Brent have been best friends since kindergarten. Now that they're in high school, they're drifting apart. It's not because they're in different classes, it's because Brent has noticed some changes in Jason. His grades have slipped, he's moody, he doesn't talk to his old friends, and he rarely shows up for practice. Brent is aware that Jason has been doing drugs and he's worried that Jason has become addicted.

When we think of addiction, we usually think of alcohol or illegal drugs. But people become addicted to medications, cigarettes, even glue

Defining an addiction is tricky, and knowing how to handle one is even harder – keep reading to find out more about addiction.

What are substance abuse and addiction?

The difference between substance abuse and addiction is very slight. Addiction begins as abuse, or using a substance like marijuana or cocaine. You can abuse a drug (or alcohol) without having an addiction. For

example, just because Sara smoked weed a few times doesn't mean that she has an addiction, but it does mean that she's abusing a drug – and that could lead to an addiction.

People can get addicted to all sorts of substances. When we think of addiction, we usually think of alcohol or illegal drugs. But people become addicted to medications, cigarettes, even glue! And some substances are more addictive than others: drugs like crack or heroin are so addictive that they may only be used once or twice before the user loses control.

Addiction means a person has no control over whether he or she uses a drug or drinks. A person who's addicted to cocaine has grown so used to the drug that he or she *has* to have it. Addiction can be physical, psychological, or both.

Physical addiction is when a person's body actually becomes

dependent on a particular substance (even smoking is physically addictive). It also means that a person builds tolerance to that substance, so that person needs a larger dose than ever before to get the same effects. When a person who is physically addicted stops using a substance like drugs, alcohol, or cigarettes, he or she may experience withdrawal symptoms. Withdrawal can be like having the flu – common symptoms are diarrhoea, shaking, and generally feeling awful.

Psychological addiction happens when the cravings for a drug are psychological or emotional. People who are psychologically addicted feel overcome by the desire to have a drug. They may lie or steal to get it.

A person crosses the line between abuse and addiction when he or she is no longer trying the drug to have fun or get high, but because he or she has come to depend on it. His or her whole life centres around the need for the drug. An addicted person – whether it's a physical or psychological addiction or both – no longer has a choice in taking a substance.

People who are psychologically addicted feel overcome by the desire to have a drug. They may lie or steal to get it

---

Signs of addiction

The most obvious sign of an addiction is the need to have a particular drug or substance. However, there are many other signs that can suggest a possible addiction, such as changes in mood or weight loss or gain. (These are also signs of other conditions, too, though, such as depression or eating disorders.)

Signs that you or someone you know may have a drug or alcohol addiction include:

Psychological signals

- use of drugs or alcohol as a way to forget problems or to relax
- withdrawal or keeping secrets from family and friends
- loss of interest in activities that used to be important
- problems with schoolwork, such as slipping grades or absences
- changes in friendships, such as hanging out only with friends who use drugs
- spending a lot of time figuring out how to get drugs
- stealing or selling belongings to be able to afford drugs
- failed attempts to stop taking drugs or drinking
- anxiety, anger, or depression
- mood swings.

Physical signals

- changes in sleeping habits
- feeling shaky or sick when trying to stop
- needing to take more of the substance to get the same effect
- changes in eating habits, including weight loss or gain.

Getting help

If you think you are addicted to drugs or alcohol, recognising that you have a problem is the first step in getting help.

A lot of people think they can kick the problem on their own, but that doesn't work for most people. Find someone you trust to talk to. It may help to talk to a friend or someone your own age at first, but a supportive and understanding adult is your best option for getting help. If you can't talk to your parents, you may want to approach a school counsellor, relative, doctor, favourite teacher, or religious leader.

Unfortunately, overcoming addiction is not easy. Quitting drugs or drinking is probably going to be the hardest thing you've ever done. It's not a sign of weakness if you need professional help from a trained drug counsellor or therapist. Most people

---

Know the signs of drug taking

Information from the Metropolitan Police

It is often difficult to tell if someone is using drugs as different substances can affect people in different ways.

Below are some of the signs to look for, although they are not absolute proof of drug use. Some of these could simply be normal signs of growing up:

- sudden changes in mood and behaviour from happy and energetic to moody and irritable
- secretiveness
- deceitfulness
- depression
- loss of appetite
- stealing money or goods
- excessive spending or borrowing money.

How to recognise the drugs

There is no easy way to identify illegal substances except by analysis. However, signs to look out for can include:

- small plastic or elaborately folded paper wraps
- burnt foil and spoons, syringes and small bottles
- a herbal substance or a solid, crumbly brown resin
- shredded cigarettes
- unusual pills, powders or liquids in small quantities
- strong, sickly sweet, smoky smell.

■ The above information is reprinted with kind permission from the Metropolitan Police. Visit www.met.police.uk for more information.

© *Metropolitan Police*

---

who try to kick a drug or alcohol addiction need professional assistance or treatment programmes to do so.

Once you start a treatment programme, try these tips to make the road to recovery less bumpy:

■ Tell your friends about your decision to stop using drugs. Your true friends will respect your decision. This may mean that you need to find a new group of friends who will be 100% supportive. Unless everyone decides to kick their drug habit at once, you probably won't be able to hang out with the friends you did drugs with before.

A lot of people think they can kick the problem on their own, but that doesn't work for most people

■ Ask your friends or family to be available when you need them. You may need to call someone in the middle of the night just to talk. If you're going through a tough time, don't try to handle things on your own – accept the help your family and friends offer.

■ Accept only invitations to events that you know won't involve drugs or alcohol. Going to the movies is probably safe, but you may want to skip a Friday night party until you're feeling more secure. Plan activities that don't involve drugs. Go to the movies, try bowling, or take an art class with a friend.

■ Have a plan about what you'll do if you find yourself in a place with

Staying clean

Recovering from a drug or alcohol addiction doesn't end with a 6-week treatment programme. It's a lifelong process. Many people find that joining a support group can help them stay clean. There are support groups specifically for teens and younger people. You'll meet people who have gone through the same experiences you have, and you'll be able to participate in real-life discussions about drugs that you won't hear in your school's health class.

Many people find that helping others is also the best way to help themselves. Your understanding of how difficult the recovery process can be will help you to support others – both teens and adults – who are battling an addiction.

If you do have a relapse, recognising the problem as soon as possible is critical. Get help right away so that you don't undo all the hard work you put into your initial recovery. And don't ever be afraid to ask for help!

drugs or alcohol. The temptation will be there sometimes, but if you know how you're going to handle it, you'll be OK. Establish a plan with your parents or siblings so that if you call home using a code, they'll know that your call is a signal you need a ride out of there.

■ Remind yourself that having an addiction doesn't make you bad or weak. If you backslide a bit, talk to an adult as soon as possible. There's nothing to be ashamed about, but it's important to get help soon so that all of the hard work you put into your recovery is not lost.

If you're worried about a friend who has an addiction, use these tips to help him or her, too. For example, let your friend know that you are available to talk or offer your support. If you notice a friend backsliding, talk about it openly and ask what

you can do to help. If your friend is going back to drugs or drinking and won't accept your help, don't be afraid to talk to a nonthreatening, understanding adult, like your parent or school counsellor. It may seem like you're ratting your friend out, but it's the best support you can offer.

Above all, offer a friend who's battling an addiction lots of encouragement and praise. It may seem corny, but hearing that you care is just the kind of motivation your friend needs.

■ This information was provided by KidsHealth, one of the largest resources online for medically reviewed health information for parents, kids and teens. For more articles like this one, visit their websites at www.teenshealth.org or www.kidshealth.org
© 1995-2005. *The Nemours Foundation*

Qualities of drugs and their potential to lead to addictiveness

	Drug	Speedy effect?	Intense effect?	Short-lasting effect?	Physical withdrawal symptoms?	Potential addictiveness
VERY ADDICTIVE	Heroin	✔ ✔ ✔ ✔ ✔	✔ ✔ ✔ ✔	✔ ✔	✔ ✔ ✔ ✔ ✔	✔ ✔ ✔ ✔ ✔
	Crack	✔ ✔ ✔ ✔ ✔	✔ ✔ ✔ ✔ ✔	✔ ✔ ✔ ✔ ✔	✔	✔ ✔ ✔ ✔ ✔
	Cocaine	✔ ✔ ✔ ✔	✔ ✔ ✔	✔ ✔ ✔ ✔	✔	✔ ✔ ✔
	Amphetamines	✔ ✔ ✔ ✔	✔ ✔ ✔	✔ ✔ ✔ ✔	✔	✔ ✔ ✔
	Tobacco	✔ ✔ ✔ ✔ ✔	✔	✔ ✔ ✔	✔	✔ ✔ ✔
	Methadone	✔ ✔	✔ ✔	✔	✔ ✔ ✔ ✔ ✔	✔ ✔ ✔
	Alcohol	✔ ✔	✔	✔ ✔	✔ ✔ ✔ ✔	✔ ✔ ✔
	Ecstasy	✔	✔ ✔ ✔	✔ ✔	✔	✔ ✔
	Cannabis	✔ ✔ ✔	✔	✔ ✔	✔	✔ ✔
HARDLY ADDICTIVE	LSD	✔	✔ ✔ ✔			✔

Sources: Team analysis based on: National Institute of Drug Abuse, USA; 'Heroin and related opiates', D. Nutt 2002; Maudsley Hospital cocaine user records; Drugs Dilemma and Choices, Royal College of Psychiatrists 2000; HIT, Liverpool, 2001; 'Cannabis and Ecstasy: Soft Drugs?' L. Iversen; and others. Chart taken from SU Drugs Report, Crown copyright.

Quarter of 15-year-olds have tried cannabis

Children are 10 times more likely to be using soft drugs than 20 years ago, a new survey has found.

Research suggests that more than a quarter of those aged 14 and 15 have tried cannabis. Six to seven per cent of children aged 12 to 13 had used the drug.

The figures also show a startling rise in the use of cannabis among younger schoolchildren.

The survey, conducted by the independent research body the Schools Health Education Unit, asked pupils in a number of different education authorities to fill out anonymous questionnaires.

Children are 10 times more likely to be using soft drugs than 20 years ago, a new survey has found

The rolling project has interviewed around 400,000 pupils since 1987 and is one of the few large-scale studies to look at drug use so far back.

David Regis, the research manager at the SHEU, said yesterday (5 June 2005): 'The results are striking. They suggest that cannabis is freely

By Duncan Gardham

available to many young people outside school.

'There was a brief levelling off in the mid-1990s but it is now climbing again. The only cheerful note is that use of the drug is now lower than the number who are receiving offers of drugs, suggesting that many are saying "no".'

There was little difference between boys and girls using drugs, with 26 per cent of boys aged 14 and 15 saying they had tried cannabis at least once and 27 per cent of girls, both up from two per cent in 1987.

For the 12- and 13-year-old age group the figures rose from one per cent to seven per cent for boys and from zero to six per cent for girls over the same period.

However, there has been a fall in the use of ecstasy and amphetamines since the mid-1990s.

6 June 2005

© Telegraph Group Limited 2005

The facts

- The Department of Health estimates that 47% of 15-year-olds have drunk alcohol in the last week, and 22% have used an illegal drug
- at least one million children in the UK are living in a family home where problematic alcohol use is an issue
- 27% of 11- to 15-year-olds have used an illicit drug in the last month
- approximately 300,000 children live in a home where heroin or crack is used (3% of all children)
- 35% of all child protection enquiries feature heroin or crack
- up to 50% of all crime is drug-related
- secondary school age children, particularly older children, are commonly offered illegal drugs. Children who do not themselves use drugs or alcohol are quite likely to know someone who does
- over 500,000 ecstasy tablets are taken every weekend, an increasing amount taken by children and young people
- one in twelve of 12-year-olds have tried drugs at least once: this increases to one in three of 14-year-olds and two in five of 16-year-olds
- Re-Solv, a campaign and education group funded by the solvents industry, estimates that a third of all volatile substance-related deaths occur the first time the substance is used – casualties are virtually all children
- some police forces estimate that up to 70% of all crime is drug or alcohol related. It is estimated that alcohol is a feature in 80% of incidences of domestic violence, and 40% of child abuse.

- The above information is reprinted with kind permission from Barnardo's. Visit www.barnardos.org.uk for more information or see page 41 for contact details.

© Barnardo's

Drug use and the young

Survey on drug use among young people in England in 2004

The survey provides estimates of the prevalence of drug use in 2004. The main findings include:

- In 2004, 10% of pupils had taken drugs in the last month. This was a decrease from 12% recorded each year from 2001 to 2003. Similarly, 18% of pupils had taken drugs in the last year, down from 21% in 2003.
- The prevalence of taking drugs in the last year and the last month was slightly higher among boys than girls. In 2004, 18% of boys had taken drugs in the last year and 11% in the last month. Equivalent figures for girls were 17% and 9%. This difference was found in earlier surveys.
- As in previous years, the prevalence of drug taking in the last year increased with age, from 5% of 11-year-olds to 32% of 15-year-olds.
- One per cent of pupils said they took drugs most days, a further 1% took drugs at least once a week, and a further 3% took drugs at least once a month.

Findings on taking individual drugs include:

- In 2004, as in previous years of the survey, pupils were far more likely to take cannabis than any other drug. Eleven per cent of pupils aged 11-15 had taken cannabis in the last year, compared with 13% each year from 2003, 2002 and 2001. Prevalence of taking cannabis in the last year was slightly higher among boys (12%) than girls (10%), and also increased sharply with age: 1% of 11-year-olds had taken the drug in the last year compared with 26% of 15-year-olds.
- Six per cent reported taking volatile substances such as gas, glue, aerosols or solvents in the last year in 2004, compared with 8% in 2003 and 6% in 2002.
- Three percent reported sniffing poppers in the last year in 2004,

broadly consistent with the proportion found in 2003 and 2002.

- Among 11- and 12-year-olds, misuse of volatile substances such as gas, glue, aerosols or solvents in the last year was more common than taking cannabis, following the trend seen in previous years. Four per cent of 11-year-olds had sniffed volatile substances in the last year and 1% had taken cannabis. The equivalent figures for 12-year-olds were 5% and 2%.
- The prevalence of Class A drug use in the last year (4%) has remained stable since 2001. In the last year, 1% of 11 to 15-year-olds had taken heroin and 1% had taken cocaine.

Pupils were also asked about which drugs they had ever been offered:

- Thirty-six per cent of pupils had ever been offered one or more drugs, a sharp decrease from 42% in 2003.
- Overall, boys were more likely than girls to have been offered

drugs (39% compared with 34%).

- Cannabis was the drug pupils were most likely to have ever been offered: 25% said they had ever been offered cannabis, down from 27% in 2003.
- In 2004, 14% of pupils said that they had ever been offered volatile substances to inhale or sniff.
- The likelihood of having ever been offered drugs increased with age, from 14% of 11-year-olds to 62% of 15-year-olds.

- This information is taken from the headline figures of the *Smoking, Drinking and Drug Use among Young People in England in 2004* report, carried out by the National Centre for Social Research/National Foundation for Educational Research published March 2004, revised April 2005. For notes on these figures or to read the full report, visit the Department of Health website at www.dh.gov.uk

© NCSR/NFER

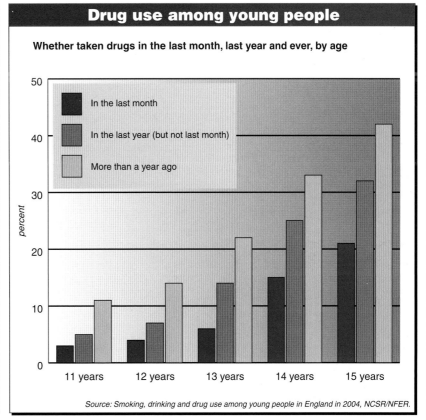

Drug use among young people

Whether taken drugs in the last month, last year and ever, by age

- In the last month
- In the last year (but not last month)
- More than a year ago

Source: Smoking, drinking and drug use among young people in England in 2004, NCSR/NFER.

Cheap as chocolate

Children binge on ecstasy as the price falls to 50p a tablet, warn drug workers

The price of ecstasy has plunged to 50p a tablet in some areas, it emerged yesterday (11 May 2005).

Children as young as eight are able to get their hands on the drug for little more than the price of a bar of chocolate.

Last night charity and youth workers revealed the fall in price meant some users were bingeing on ecstasy.

They were swallowing as many as 20 tablets a day, often after buying them in the school playground.

Children as young as eight are able to get their hands on ecstasy for little more than the price of a bar of chocolate

The escalating problem was revealed by the drugs charity Lifeline after discussions with youth workers.

Spokesman Michael Linnell said: 'Taking ecstasy seems to have moved away from the club scene. Some people are taking pills all day long, using ten to 20 pills a day.

'It is also coming up that more and more young people between the ages of 12 and 15, and occasionally much younger, are taking ecstasy on a daily basis.

'We have had cases of eight-year-olds taking ecstasy. Young people die from ecstasy.

'Drug workers have even reported that pills can be bought for as little as 50p each.'

Mr Linnell added: 'This is not about evil dealers hanging around the school gates – that would be easy to detect. It is other young people supplying their friends. Nine out of ten youngsters do not buy from dealers but from their friends.

'We do not know what is in these pills. When ecstasy first came on to the market it was quite pure, but it has become less and less so.'

By Ben Taylor,
Crime Correspondent

Six schoolgirls were taken to hospital last December after they were supplied with ecstasy by another pupil at Witton Park High in Blackburn. They were believed to have paid 50p each for the drugs.

Local youth worker Nick Stephenson said yesterday: 'We have been saying for years that ecstasy is no longer at £10 or £20 a tablet but much nearer £1 or £2.

'We have even heard of it going for as little as 50p a pill. It is not surprising, therefore, that young people are getting hold of it.'

An estimated 430,000 people in Britain take ecstasy regularly, with up to two million tablets consumed every weekend.

As the strength of the drug – known scientifically as MDMA – has declined, the quantity taken by users has sharply increased.

Last night anti-ecstasy campaigner Paul Betts, whose daughter Leah died after taking the drug in 1995, warned youngsters they were dicing with death.

The former policeman said: 'It is worrying that younger people seem to be targeted by dealers and it is all because older people have started to say no. There needs to be much more education from both schools and parents for younger children so they are aware of the dangers of drugs like ecstasy.'

Observers say many more youngsters would have died if they were taking 20 pills of pure ecstasy. But they warned that one pill, no matter how impure, could be enough to kill in some cases.

Ecstasy, which exploded onto the nightclub scene in the late 1980s, once cost as much as £25 a tablet. Two years ago, pills were available for £2.50 and the price has been falling ever since. By 2004, it was £1 a time. The drug is believed to be

responsible for more than 200 deaths in the last 15 years as it has spawned a huge industry, producing millions of pills a year.

Lifeline, which is based in the North-West of England, say the 50p price tag is being quoted in Lancashire.

Detective Superintendent Bob Helm, of the county's police, said: 'There is a message here for parents and those who work with children that if they do come across what they suspect might be ecstasy or any form of tablets they should do something about it by contacting the police.' A spokesman for the Government drugs information line Talk to FRANK said the reports from drug workers were worrying.

But he added: 'The usual price for ecstasy is somewhere between £2 and £5 and it is unlikely anyone paying a price as low as 50p is getting proper ecstasy.'

Michele Elliott, of the children's charity Kidscape, said: 'This is absolutely horrific. We are going to have children dying.

'We have got to make sure that schools and parents know what is going on. And we have got to warn these kids of the very real risks they face.'

■ This article first appeared in the *Daily Mail*, 12 May 2005.

One in seven young drivers drive on drugs

Information from Brake

More than one in seven (14%) young drivers aged 17-25 admit putting lives at risk by driving after taking illegal drugs, according to a survey of 1,150 young people by Brake, the national road safety charity.[1]

Of those who admitted driving on drugs, one in ten said they did so after consuming alcohol as well – a particularly lethal combination. It is likely that even more young drivers drive on drugs, as some drivers surveyed are likely to have failed to admit their law-breaking.

Young people are not only putting their own lives at risk, but those of their young passengers and other road users. Nearly nine in ten of the young drug-drivers surveyed said they carry passengers when driving on drink or drugs.

Brake
the road safety charity
www.brake.org.uk

A huge proportion of drivers killed on our roads are young – one in four car drivers who die behind the wheel are under 25, despite this age group accounting for just one in fifteen car licence-holders.[2] Last year, road deaths overall fell by 8%, yet deaths among 16- to 19-year-old drivers and passengers rose by 12%.[3]

The survey results come just days after a coroner branded drivers who have smoked cannabis as even more dangerous than drunk-drivers, while speaking at the inquest of a four-year-old who was killed by a 19-year-old driver who had smoked cannabis. Isabella Hill died after Barnaby Pearce crashed into her grandfather's car at nearly 80mph – he had smoked two joints earlier that day. The coroner pointed out that cannabis distorts a driver's perception of speed and their ability to react.[4]

A study carried out on behalf of the Government shows driving on illegal drugs has increased massively over past decades and is now endemic in our society – 18% of drivers who died behind the wheel 1996-2000 had illegal drugs in their system, compared to 3% during the period 1985-1988.[5] The latest figures from the study are due to be released later this year.

Claire Brixey's son, Ashley, was killed in October 2004 aged 20 while travelling as a passenger in his friend's car. His friend had been drinking and taking drugs. Claire says: 'Ashley had his whole life ahead of him and this was snatched away because his friend decided to get behind the wheel after drinking and taking drugs – a deliberate decision that put his own life and his passengers' lives at risk. It's difficult to put into words the pain that Ashley's death has caused, but I hope that other young people will realise the devastation caused to my family by drugged driving, and make a decision never to do it themselves.'

Barbara Pearce was seriously injured in a head-on crash with a car driven by a young man who had alcohol, cocaine, cannabis and ecstasy in his system. The driver, 21, and his passenger, 25, were both killed. Barbara suffered full penetrative burns and fractured every bone from the pelvis down. Barbara says: 'I used to be a professional teacher. Now I'm a professional hospital patient thanks to a drunk and drugged driver. I would urge anyone considering driving after drinking or taking drugs to think about the damage you could do to yourself or someone else in a crash – you might think it's boring to stay sober, but imagine how boring it is never being able to walk or move about.'

Mary Williams OBE, chief executive of Brake, says: 'It's high time that young people were made to realise the horrific consequences of drink and drugged driving. Through our helpline, Brake frequently supports families whose loved ones have been killed suddenly and violently because a driver has decided to get behind the wheel on drink or drugs. It's a disgrace that so many young people are taking these risks and an outrage that the Government does not do more to raise awareness among this age group and invest more in policing our roads.'

Brake provides free volunteer-led presentations to young people in schools, colleges and youth groups. Volunteers are trained by the FedEx & Brake Road Safety Academy, funded by express delivery company FedEx to deliver hard-hitting presentations to groups of young people on the potential consequences of drink or drugged driving, speeding and not belting up. Many volunteers have been affected by death or injury on the roads and talk about their personal experiences. Youth workers, educators and volunteers interested in getting involved in the scheme can call Brake on 01484 559909, email iwanttohelp@brake.org.uk, or go to www.brake.org.uk.

Brake has also produced a FREE leaflet on the dangers of drink and drugged driving, funded by the Department for Transport. These are available to driving instructors and other professionals who work with young drivers. Call 01484 559909 to order.

Brake is calling on the Government to take the following action to tackle deaths and injuries involving young drugged-drivers:

- Increased investment in advertising, including year-round prime-time TV advertising on the dangers of drink and drugged driving, targeting young people.
- Increased powers for police to carry out random, targeted testing for drink and drugs at the roadside, such as at drink and drug drive hotspots at pub and club closing times.
- Increased numbers of traffic police, to allow random roadside testing and an increased police presence on the roads.
- Roll out training of police to ensure Field Impairment Tests can be carried out at the roadside across the UK.
- Introduce a type-approved electronic drug-testing device that can be used at the roadside.
- Introduce a 'graduated' driving licence, including a post-test period lasting a year, during which newly-qualified drivers are not allowed to carry more than one passenger, drive at night or on motorways, or drive vehicles with high-capacity engines, without supervision from a qualified driving instructor, and must display a 'P' plate.

Notes

1 Survey of 1,150 17- to 25-year-olds in full-time education by Brake
2 Figures provided by the Driver and Vehicle Licensing Agency, based on a 2002 census
3 Department for Transport figures, 2005
4 Metro, Friday, 12 August 2005
5 Study by TRL on behalf of the Department for Transport

■ The above information is reprinted with kind permission from Brake, the road safety charity. Visit www.brake.org.uk for more information or see page 41 for details.

© Brake

Young drug users feel neglected by parents

Information from the British Psychological Society

Previous studies have shown that parental control and the amount of parental warmth are key factors in the kinds of deviant adolescent behaviour associated with drug abuse and other criminal activities. New research shows that such factors may also be extremely important in adolescents who go on to become users of ecstasy.

Researcher Catharine Montgomery, Dr John Fisk and Dr Russell Newcombe from Liverpool John Moores University will present the findings of their study at the British Psychological Society's Annual Conference at the University of Manchester on Thursday 31 March 2005.

The researchers investigated parenting style in a group of regular ecstasy users. They predicted that such users would have been raised by parents whom they perceived to be indulgent, show a lack of control and be neglectful.

85 ecstasy users who had been taking the drug for two years and 83 non-users completed a questionnaire on parenting style (including questions such as 'How late were you allowed to stay out on a school night?' and 'How often do your parents spend time just talking to you?') and two intelligence tests. In addition they were asked about their education and frequency and intensity of ecstasy and other drug use.

As predicted the team found that ecstasy users scored significantly lower on the two dimensions of the parenting style questionnaire (acceptance/involvement and strictness/supervision) suggesting that they perceived their parents to have low control, and to lack warmth in their interactions with them, which points to a neglectful parenting style.

While there were no significant differences between the groups in educational background and intelligence, ecstasy users did score significantly lower on some memory tests.

This study supports other research which has shown that the children of parents who demonstrate little control or warmth are more likely to use drugs. The research team noted that 'The results of the study do not necessarily mean that the parents of drug users are neglecting their children, but the finding that they are perceived this way is highly significant, and quite worrying.'

1 April 2005

■ The above information is reprinted with kind permission from the British Psychological Society. Visit www.bps.org.uk for more information.

© British Psychological Society

Drugs and the family

Family study reveals the devastating impact of problem drug users on brothers, sisters and parents

'For ten years our life got kinda took away from us. I felt we were in a big hole hangin' on to the sides... I was powerless... I couldnae change it, I couldnae make it better.'
Mick, drug user's father, interviewed in Glasgow.

Drug treatment and prevention services have concentrated on problem users while overlooking the serious damage caused to their families – including younger brothers and sisters who are at added risk of developing drug problems themselves.

Drugs in the family, a new report for the Joseph Rowntree Foundation, exposes the devastating impact that an individual's heroin or crack-cocaine habit often has on other family members. Based on in-depth interviews with drugs users, their parents and younger siblings, it reveals how families are drawn into a downward spiral of problems. These include:

- Stress, anxiety and related health problems through trying to protect the family member from harm – including bitter family rows over how best to respond.
- Parents lacking the time or energy

to support their other children as their child with the drug problem increasingly absorbs their attention.

- Stealing by drug users from family members to fund their habit.
- Brothers and sisters losing a valued relationship with a sibling whose drug obsession has made them self-centred, argumentative and unreliable.
- Routine exposure to drug-taking at home. While some brothers and sisters in the study were deterred by what they saw, others had been encouraged to experiment themselves.

Marina Barnard, a Research Fellow at the University of Glasgow's Centre for Drug Misuse Research and the study's author, said: 'Research for more than a decade has highlighted the danger that young people will be initiated into drugs like heroin and cocaine by an older brother or sister, yet the risks have not been properly acknowledged by policy makers or by treatment and prevention agencies. Some younger brothers and sisters in this study saw their siblings as sad, angry people who were being destroyed by their drug habit, but others had either become curious enough to experiment with drugs themselves or been deliberately encouraged to try them.'

The research in Glasgow found parents were almost always thrown into shock and disarray by the discovery that one or more children had developed a problem with drugs. Typical first responses were confusion, panic and a sense of shame that deterred them from seeking help from outside agencies.

As unsuccessful attempts to cope led families into deeper difficulties, younger brothers and sisters were increasingly drawn into the conflict: mediating between their parents and their drug-user sibling, and trying to prevent goods and money being stolen from the house.

Family support groups were rarely accessed until families had been living with the drug problem for many years. However, parents who had joined a local group said they found it valuable and felt less isolated. Some support groups offered breaks for families to obtain some much-needed respite from the problems at home. However, the report points out that support groups are often short-lived as a result of being informal and self-funded.

Marina Barnard said: 'The problem drug use of a close family member creates enduring stress, anxiety and conflict that have long-term consequences and severely affect the health and well-being of parents, brothers and sisters. Yet this study underlines the real difficulties in trying to help families, given that they tend to focus on the drug-affected child, rather than the negative effects on themselves.

'We need to respond to the challenge with compassion and imagination. Policy makers must give careful thought to ways in which better family support can most effectively mesh with existing treatment and prevention services. More effort could be made to help families when they first find out about the drug use, before the problems become intractable. Mentoring programmes could also play a part in enabling younger brothers and sisters to resist becoming problem drug users themselves.'

- The above information is reprinted with kind permission from the Joseph Rowntree Foundation. Visit www.jrf.org.uk for more information.
© Joseph Rowntree Foundation

Random drug tests for pupils at start of new school term

By David Sapsted

Pupils starting the new term at one secondary school yesterday (5 January 2005) became the first to face a new test – for drugs.

Despite criticism that the scheme, which is backed by the Prime Minister, violated civil liberties and could lead to truancy, the Abbey School in Faversham, Kent, became the first state school in the country to introduce the random tests.

Martin Barnes, the chief executive of DrugScope, has given warning that testing risks driving drug use further underground and may increase truancies

Ten pupils, aged between 11 and 18, had their names randomly selected by computer yesterday morning to undergo the tests, which involved mouth swabs being taken by specially trained, non-teaching members of staff.

Results will be available in three days to show if any of the children have taken cocaine, cannabis or ecstasy.

Peter Walker, the headmaster, who introduced the tests in an attempt to stop children experimenting with drugs, expects that up to 20 out of the school's 960 pupils will be tested during a normal week.

'None of the pupils will be forced to take a test against their wishes,' he said.

'If they refuse, we will call the parents in to the school and discuss it. It might indicate that the child has been taking some stuff and doesn't want to be found out.'

So far, only 15 per cent of the 701 parents who have returned authorisation forms have refused to allow their child to be tested. Mr Walker said no pupil would be expelled if he or she had a positive test.

'It's not a question of punishment, it's a question of support,' he said.

'We will decide whether they need counselling, police support or health care. We do not have a bigger drugs problem than any other school. There's a chance we have even less of a problem because we are so pro-active.'

Last February, in an interview with a tabloid newspaper that is sponsoring the Faversham tests, Tony Blair gave his blessing to random drug testing in schools.

There has been evidence from America that such tests can reduce drug-taking while, in Britain, a recent survey found that almost a third of 11- to 15-year-olds questioned said they had tried illicit drugs.

However, drug tests have drawn criticism from educationists and civil rights groups. Martin Barnes, the chief executive of DrugScope, who sits on the Government's advisory council on the misuse of drugs, has given warning that testing risks driving drug use further underground and may increase truancies.

'We do not accept that testing pupils as young as 11 is a proportionate response to general concerns about drug use,' he said.

Barry Hugill, a spokesman for Liberty, said: 'We're not at all sure what this is going to achieve apart from turning perfectly innocent children into supposed drug abusers.

If they refuse to be tested, the implication is obvious: they've got something to hide.'

Zack Kirby, 16, who lives in Faversham, is one pupil whose parents have refused permission for him to take part in the testing.

He said: 'I don't agree with it. It's an invasion of privacy. It should be up to your mum and dad to sort this kind of thing out.'

While some private schools have already introduced testing, no other state schools have yet committed themselves to a regular programme of tests. The Scottish Executive has consistently opposed such schemes in schools north of the border.

6 January 2005

Dangerous highs

The hidden solvent abuse among children and young people

Volatile substance abuse (VSA) is responsible for more deaths among children aged 10 to 16 in the UK than illegal drugs, yet the problem remains hidden owing to prejudice and a lack of public awareness.

Dangerous Highs, a joint report from the National Children's Bureau (NCB) and ChildLine, published on Wednesday 22 June 2005, reveals that children as young as 10 are inhaling solvents and flirting with death on a regular basis.

The report, which analyses over 350 calls made to ChildLine about VSA, shows that volatile substances are not used simply to get high. Often there are severe traumas as well as emotional and mental health problems that go unsupported and cause children to abuse volatile substances as a means of escape.

The accessibility of products found in every home in the country such as glue, paint, correcting fluid and nail varnish means VSA often begins at an early age, with children constantly finding new products to abuse. A girl sniffing nail varnish to block out the pain of her parents' beatings and a boy 'buzzing' deodorant in a desperate attempt to fit in are among the experiences described to ChildLine counsellors. The report also shows that children already marginalised by society – such as children in care or in young offenders' institutes – are particularly vulnerable to VSA.

The hidden and taboo nature of

VSA is reinforced in *Dangerous Highs*. Children describe feeling scared and ashamed of their abuse of solvents. They therefore often use them alone where, if something goes wrong, there is a high chance death can occur as there is noone around to help.

Report author Simon Blake, assistant director of children's development at NCB, says: 'In the 1980s everyone knew about the problem of glue sniffing but over the last 20 years it has slowly slipped from public view and has been forgotten. Yet VSA continues to cause death and harm to many. With children playing Russian roulette with their lives it is no longer tenable to ignore VSA.'

ChildLine chief executive Carole Easton says: 'The accounts of children who call ChildLine about VSA are difficult and painful to read. It is crucial that we face up to the fact that children are abusing volatile

---

Solvents

How they work

Solvents come in glues, cleaning fluids, aerosols, petrol, Tipp-Ex, paint, varnish, nail polish, dyes, fire extinguishers and room fresheners. Solvent names include toluene, benzene, xylene and acetone. Some of these are poisonous, especially benzene which can cause leukaemia.

When you sniff them, they come into contact with air, and partly turn into gases or tiny droplets. These gases whizz from your lungs into the blood and quickly into the brain, making you feel out of it for a while. The active chemicals disappear from your blood several hours after the last sniff as the chemicals are broken down in your liver.

What the law says

Although it is not illegal to sniff solvents, it is illegal to sell them to young people. The Intoxicating Substances Supply Act (1985) made it an offence to supply someone under the age of 18 yrs with a substance known to 'achieve intoxication', i.e. get you high.

History factoid

The Victorians used to advertise laughing gas nights at the theatre – you could pay to watch sniffers giggling, falling over and fighting. Nowadays we just have Jerry Springer...

Amazing thing about it

Many sniffers end up in hospital not because of the poisonous fumes, but because they set fire to themselves – solvents are very flammable.

■ The above information is reprinted with kind permission from Doctor Ann. Visit www.doctorann.org for more information or see page 41.

© Teenage Health Websites Ltd

---

substances to escape the pain their lives are causing them. ChildLine and NCB hope that publishing the *Dangerous Highs* report will put VSA back on the public agenda; these desperate and despairing young people driven to risk their health and lives deserve nothing less.'

NCB and ChildLine are calling for a range of measures including:

- Legislation to minimise quantity of dangerous solvents in products.
- Continued work to regulate and reduce the supply of volatile substances.
- Emotional help for vulnerable children and young people, tackling the real issues behind their despair before volatile substances are even considered. Professionals to be aware of the

support available to those who do abuse volatile substances.

- Education on VSA to be included in drug education in schools and other settings – particularly those where vulnerable children and young people are living, such as YOI and residential homes.
- Education for parents and carers so they can identify VSA and feel confident in talking about it and the underlying reasons why it may occur.

Note

Volatile substances include hair-spray, glue, nail varnish remover, deodorant, various aerosols and solvents. At 15% of all 15- to 16-year-olds the UK has the highest level of solvent use in the EU.

Resources

- Spotlight Briefing – Teaching and learning about volatile substance abuse (http://www.ncb.org.uk/resources/res_detail.asp?id=692)
- 'Dangerous Highs' (http://www.ncb.org.uk/resources/res_detail.asp?id=837)
- Cards for Life (http://www.ncb-books.org.uk/NCB_Books_New_releases_20.html)

22 June 2005

- The above information is reprinted with kind permission from the National Children's Bureau. Please visit www.ncb.org.uk for more information, or if you wish to write to them, see page 41 for their address details.

© NCB

In their words

The hidden victims of substance misuse. Katie's story (age five)

When Katie was three, she often went hungry. But no one noticed. She often cried. But no one heard. That's what it's like being the child of drug-dependent parents.

Katie's seen things no child should ever have to. She's seen her dad go for her mum with a pair of scissors. She's seen strangers kicking down the door and demanding money.

Katie often cried. But no one heard. That's what it's like being the child of drug-dependent parents

---

She's had to learn to look after herself. To get herself dressed in the morning and to find her own food. By the time she was just four years old she was not just taking care of herself, but also her baby sister, Hannah. Looking after a two-year-old is hard work for most adults. Imagine what it is like for a four-year-old.

Barnardo's
GIVING CHILDREN BACK THEIR FUTURE

Then one day her dad was imprisoned for drug-related offences. This turned out to be the best thing that ever happened to Katie. Away from her partner's influence, Katie's mum Susan was able to come off drugs, at least for long enough to realise that this was no life for her or the girls. Desperate to do the right thing for her children, she contacted a health worker who referred them to Akwaaba – one of Barnardo's projects based in Deptford, south-east London.

Katie now had somewhere safe to go – even if just for a few hours a day. But she had massive problems when she came to Akwaaba. A timid, frail figure, she flinched every time someone brushed past her. It will

take a lot of patience and care to rebuild her life. But she is making progress.

Thanks to Akwaaba, Katie's had a glimpse of what life is like for other four-year-olds – a life of learning instead of violence and fear. Of course, it will take years to rebuild her life. None of her problems are solved, or forgotten, but at least now she has a chance!

- The above information is reprinted with kind permission from Barnardo's. For more information visit www.barnardos.org.uk or see page 41 for contact details.

© Barnardo's

The score

Facts about drugs

What's the big deal...?

Everyone has something to say about drugs. Even so it's still an issue wrapped in myths, and often fiction gets in the way of facts.

Knowing the score isn't just about knowing the buzz different drugs can give. It's also about being aware of the effects they can have on your mind, your body and even the way you live your life. There are serious risks linked to drug taking, so it's vital to get your hands on information you can trust.

Different drugs have different effects

People take certain drugs to make them feel confident and excited. Others use drugs to relax them or affect the way they see things. It's impossible to accurately predict the effects of any drug. Much depends on the amount taken, the user's mood and their surroundings. However, some drugs can be divided into broad groups:

Stimulants

Drugs which act on the central nervous system and increase brain activity (cocaine; crack; ecstasy; Poppers; speed; tobacco).

Depressants

Drugs which act on the central nervous system and slow down brain activity (alcohol; gases, glues and aerosols; tranquillisers).

Hallucinogens

Drugs which act on the mind, distorting the way users see and hear things (cannabis; ketamine; LSD; magic mushrooms).

Analgesics

Drugs which have a painkilling effect (heroin).

Anabolic steroids

These drugs promote the growth of skeletal muscle and increase lean body mass.

Crucial questions

What does the picture on a tab of acid say about the trip?
Nothing!

There is NO connection between the picture and the effects of the acid tab.

In many ways, ecstasy users are human guinea pigs

Users can experience trips differently every time. The effects depend on the user's mood, where they are and who they're with at the time.

There is no way of predicting what a trip will be like.

Is cannabis safe?
You may have heard people say cannabis is risk free. This isn't true.

Heavy use of cannabis over a long period of time can lead to users relying on the drug as a way of relaxing and being sociable.

Heavy, long-term cannabis use can make you feel less energetic than normal. This can have a negative effect on the way you live your life.

Smoking cannabis with tobacco causes lung damage. In fact, it's reckoned that smoke from an unfiltered spliff carries more risks than a cigarette. However, people tend to smoke many more cigarettes than spliffs.

What are the long-term effects of taking ecstasy?
Basically no one really knows. The chemical name for ecstasy is MDMA and what we do know is that MDMA dramatically affects the brain chemistry of animals; has also been linked to liver and kidney problems; heavy long-term use may increase the chance of severe depression and other mental illnesses in later life.

In many ways, ecstasy users are human guinea pigs.

Smoking and drinking aren't illegal, so what's the problem?

OK, so you can buy cigarettes at 16, and if you're 18 the pubs can sell you alcoholic drinks, but tobacco and alcohol can be abused like any drug.

Smoke and you risk cancer, heart disease and serious lung problems.

In the UK, about 13 people die every hour because of smoking-related diseases.

Drink too much alcohol and you risk damage to the heart, liver, stomach and brain.

One thousand young people under 15 are admitted to hospital each year with acute alcohol intoxication. All need emergency treatment, many in intensive care.

When people talk about flashbacks, what do they mean?

LSD and magic mushrooms are hallucinogenic drugs – they change the way a user sees and hears things.

This is called a trip. A flashback is something that:

- can happen later – days, months, even years after taking the drug;
- is a sudden memory of something from a previous trip;
- may not last long, but can seem very real. If you're doing something like crossing a road at the time it could leave you exposed to serious danger.

All drugs carry risks

The effects may be unexpected.

Many drugs sold on the 'street' have been mixed with other substances, so users can never be sure what they're getting.

Users may become tolerant to some drugs (e.g. alcohol, heroin and speed). This means their bodies have become so used to the drug they need to take more to get the effect they want.

Users may overdose (take too much for their bodies to handle). With alcohol, heroin, gases, glues and aerosols an overdose can be fatal.

Emergency

Drugs affect everyone differently. Sometimes people suffer a bad reaction. If it all goes horribly wrong, don't be the one who stands back helpless.

Know what to do if someone:

- **Gets really drowsy**
  Calm them and be reassuring. NEVER give coffee to rouse them. If symptoms persist, place them in the recovery position. Call an ambulance if necessary.
- **Gets tense and panics**
  Calm them and be reassuring. Explain that the feelings will pass. Steer them clear of crowds, noisy music and bright lights. If they start breathing very quickly, calm them down and encourage them to take long slow breaths.
- **Gets too hot and dehydrates**
  Move them to a cooler, quiet area (outside is often best. Remove excess clothing and try to cool them down. Encourage them to sip non-alcoholic fluids such as fruit juice and isotonic sports drinks (about a pint every hour). If symptoms persist call an ambulance, but make sure someone stays with them. ECSTASY

and SPEED affect the body's temperature control. If users dance energetically without taking regular breaks or keeping up fluids, there's a real danger that their bodies could overheat and dehydrate (lose too much body fluid). Warning signs include: cramps, fainting, headache or sudden tiredness.

- **Becomes unconscious**
  Call an ambulance. Place them in the recovery position. Check breathing. Be prepared to do mouth-to-mouth resuscitation.

Keep them warm, but not too hot. If you've called an ambulance and know what drugs have been taken, always tell the crew. It might SAVE A LIFE and you won't get into trouble.

- The above information is taken from the Department of Health document *Know the Score: Facts about Drugs* and is reprinted with permission. For more information please visit the department's website at www.dh.gov.uk

© Crown copyright

Student drug use survey

Online drugs survey conducted by Student Direct, published May 2005.

Question 1: Have you ever taken any illegal drugs?
Yes - 75%

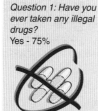

Question 2: Have you ever taken any illegal drugs (excluding cannabis)?
Yes - 47%
No - 49%
No answer - 4%

Question 3: If so, which drugs have you tried?
Ecstasy - 37%
Cocaine - 26%
Speed - 12%
Mushrooms - 12%
Ketamine - 9%
LSD - 8%
Crack - 4%

Question 4: If so, how often on average do you take drugs?
Regularly (at least monthly) - 50%
Rarely - 37%
Tried but never again - 13%

Question 5: Have you ever tried cannabis?
Yes - 72%
No - 23%
Not answered - 3%

Question 6: If so, how often do you use it?
Every day - 10%
Regularly (at least monthly) - 27%
Rarely - 24%
Tried but never again - 12%
No answer - 23%

Question 7: Why do you take drugs?
To enhance a night out - 37%
Relaxation - 31%
To fit in - 8%
No reason - 16%
Addiction - 4%

Question 8: Do you take drugs alone or with friends?
With friends - 92%

CAUTION
FRIENDS THAT DO DRUGS

Question 9: What or who is your key influence when making decisions?
Friends - 22%
Curiosity - 47%
Media - 3%
Religion - 2%
Other - 26%

Question 10: Do you think students take too many drugs?
Yes - 37%
No - 48%
No answer - 15%

Question 11: What do you think of the government's attitude to drugs?
Too strict - 32%
About right - 33%
Not strict enough - 25%

Question 12: Do you support the smoking of cannabis in public places?
Yes - 28%
No - 56%
Not answered - 16%

Question 13: Do you consider tobacco or alcohol as dangerous as illegal drugs?
Yes - 59%
No - 35%
Not answered - 6%

Source: Student Direct. Survey carried out online by Catherine Bolsover, Alex Wood and Fiona Eatwell.

The Misuse of Drugs Act 1971

Information from DrugScope

The Misuse of Drugs Act 1971 is intended to prevent the non-medical use of certain drugs. For this reason it controls not just medicinal drugs (which will also be in the Medicines Act) but also drugs with no current medical uses. Offences under this Act overwhelmingly involve the general public, and even when the same drug and a similar offence are involved, penalties are far tougher. Drugs subject to this Act are known as 'controlled' drugs. The law defines a series of offences, including unlawful supply, intent to supply, import or export (all these are collectively known as 'trafficking' offences), and unlawful production. The main difference from the Medicines Act is that the Misuse of Drugs Act also prohibits unlawful possession. To enforce this law the police have the special powers to stop, detain and search people on 'reasonable suspicion' that they are in possession of a controlled drug.

Drugs subject to the Misuse of Drugs Act 1971 are known as 'controlled' drugs

The laws controlling drug use are complicated. The Misuse of Drugs Act (MDA) regulates what are termed controlled drugs. It divides drugs into three classes as follows:

- Class A: These include cocaine and crack (a form of cocaine), ecstasy, heroin, LSD, methadone, magic mushrooms containing ester of psilocin and any Class B drug which is injected.
- Class B: These include amphetamines, barbiturates, and codeine.
- Class C: These include cannabis (in resin, oil or herbal form), amphetamines, anabolic steroids and minor tranquillisers.

Class A drugs are treated by the law as the most dangerous.

Offences under the Misuse of Drugs Act can include:

- Possession of a controlled drug.
- Possession with intent to supply another person.
- Production, cultivation or manufacture of controlled drugs.
- Supplying another person with a controlled drug.
- Offering to supply another person with a controlled drug.
- Import or export of controlled drugs.
- Allowing premises you occupy or manage to be used for the consumption of certain controlled drugs (smoking of cannabis or opium but not use of other controlled drugs) or supply or production of any controlled drug.

NB Certain controlled drugs such as amphetamines, barbiturates, methadone, minor tranquillisers and occasionally heroin can be obtained through a legitimate doctor's prescription. In such cases their possession is not illegal.

The law is even more complicated by the fact that some drugs are covered by other laws, are not covered at all or treated in an exceptional way under the Misuse of Drugs Act.

Alcohol is not illegal for an over-5-year-old to consume away from licensed premises. It is an offence for a vendor to knowingly sell to an under-18-year-old. A 14-year-old can go into a pub alone but not consume alcohol. A 16-year-old can buy and consume beer, port, cider or perry (but not spirits) in a pub if having a meal in an area set aside for this purpose. In some areas there are by-laws restricting drinking of alcohol on the streets at any age. Police also have powers to confiscate alcohol from under-18s who drink in public places.

GHB (gammahydroxybutyrate) is a colourless, odourless liquid which comes in a small bottle and has sedative and euphoric effects. It is controlled under the Misuse of Drugs Act so possession is an offence.

Ketamine usually comes as a powder. The initial rush is usually followed by feelings of dissociation and an anaesthetic type experience. It is commonly used as an animal tranquilliser and for surgery on animals. Ketamine is a not covered by the Misuse of Drugs Act and possession is not an offence. It is a prescription only medicine under the Medicines Act meaning unauthorised supply is illegal.

Khat is a plant that is grown in eastern Africa and the Arabian peninsula. Chewing the leaves has a stimulant effect. Some khat is imported to the UK and sold in greengrocers, specialist health food shops and some 'head' shops. The khat plant (the main form in which khat is sold) is not covered under the Misuse of Drugs Act and possession or supply is not an offence.

Magic mushrooms are now a Class A drug under the Drugs Act 2005: 'fungus (of any kind) which contains psilocin or an ester of psilocin'. This does not include Fly Agaric which is still legal.

Poppers (liquid gold, amyl or butyl nitrite) are not covered by the MDA and are not illegal to possess or buy. They are often sold in joke and sex shops but also in some pubs, clubs, tobacconists and sometimes music or clothes shops used by young people. Though not fully tested in court, the Medicines Control Agency has stated that poppers are regarded by them as a medicine and so fall under the Medicines Act 1968. This allows only licensed outlets, such as chemists, to sell the drug.

Solvents (aerosols, gases, glues etc.) are not illegal to possess, use or buy at any age. In England and Wales it is an offence for a shopkeeper to sell them to an under-18-year-old if they know they are to be used for intoxicating purposes. The Government has extended this legislation to make it illegal for shopkeepers to sell lighter fuel (butane) to under-18s whether or not they know it will be used for intoxicating purposes. This law came into force on 1st Oct 1999, although it was not an 'extension' to the Intoxicating Substances Supply Act, but an amendment to the Consumer Protection Act.

Anabolic steroids are controlled under the Misuse of Drugs Act as Class C drugs but their legal status is

complicated. In most situations the possession offence is waived, meaning that people who possess or use steroids without a prescription are unlikely to be prosecuted. However, in some areas of the UK police have successfully prosecuted people for possession of steroids when the steroids have not been in the form of a medicinal product. It is always an offence to sell or supply steroids to another person. People can also be prosecuted for possession with intent to supply if they have large quantities of steroids without a prescription for them.

Tobacco. It is not an offence for people of any age to purchase or use cigarettes or other tobacco products. It is an offence for a vendor to sell tobacco products to someone they know to be under 16-years-old. Police also have powers to confiscate tobacco products from under-16s who are smoking in public places.

Minor tranquillisers (librium, valium etc.) are controlled under the

Misuse of Drugs Act as Class C drugs but the possession offence is waived so that it is not illegal to possess or use them without a prescription. It is an offence to sell or supply them to another person. The exception is temazepam and rohypnol tranquillisers which are illegal to be in possession of without a prescription.

The number of persons dealt with for drugs offences fell by 15 per cent in 2000, following a fall of 6 per cent during the previous year. In total 104,400 persons were found guilty or cautioned (source *Drug Seizure and Offender Statistics 2000*). Of these people 90 per cent were male and 10 per cent were female. Offenders aged less than 21 years represented about 34 per cent of offenders in 2000 – the average age of offenders is now a little over 25 years.

Of the 104,400 people who committed drug offences under the MDA in 2000:

- 41 per cent were given a police caution and not taken to court.
- 26 per cent were fined.
- 24 per cent were dealt with by other means such as suspended prison sentences, probation or supervision orders, community service orders or discharged.
- 9 per cent were imprisoned.

What happens to people who commit drug offences varies in different parts of the UK. Police forces in some areas are more likely to caution than in other areas. Some local police forces are more likely than others to charge people and take them to court. What happens in courts also varies. Some courts are more likely to give out custodial sentences or large fines than others.

- The above information is reprinted with kind permission from DrugScope. For more information please visit www.drugscope.org.uk or see page 41 for address details.

© DrugScope

Bad deal

Recently Emma was caught by the police with some ecstasy tabs in her pocket. This is her story...

Name: Emma
Age: 16
Lives: Brighton
Occupation: Student
Criminal charge: Posession with intent to supply

'I still don't think of myself as a drug dealer'

'As I see it, dealers are big-time gangsters, or those people outside clubs trying to sell Es, trips and whizz. All I did was try to sort a few friends with ecstasy. Like I told the police, my mates asked me. I wasn't going to push it on them. In fact I thought I was doing them a favour. I even said that none of the tabs were for me, but it didn't make any difference.

Awaiting punishment

'The police haven't told me what's going to happen yet. I could get a reprimand or a warning – which means a police record. I might even have to appear in court. The fact that ecstasy is a Class A drug isn't going to help. Apparently it's the most serious drugs category of all, and can carry the heaviest penalties. Also, a lot depends on the amount of drugs the police find. I was only carrying a few Es, and I was on my own when they stopped me. Still, the police were convinced that they weren't just for my own personal use.

So disappointed

'It's been a big shock for my parents – when they turned up at the station my mum was white as a sheet. Dad wouldn't even look at me. They've said they'll stand by me, but I know they feel let down.

The future

'Word's already spreading through school. My teachers are bound to find out – and then what? What really hurts is that everyone's talking about me behind my back. No one understands how bad I feel. I wish I'd known about the risks I was taking. But it's too late now. I've just got to face what's coming.'

■ The above information is taken from the Department of Health booklet *The Score: Facts about Drugs*. To view the entire booklet or for more information, please visit the Department of Health website at www.dh.gov.uk

© Crown copyright

Drug smuggling

Information from HM Revenue and Customs

Illegal drugs can touch the lives of everyone. You might be affected directly if you have a friend or a family member who is a drug user, or indirectly through having to live with the threat of drug-related crime.

Experts estimate the worldwide illegal drugs trade is worth as much as the individual oil, gas or world tourism industries. Whatever the true figure, the UK alone spends more than one billion pounds per year tackling the problem.

We are committed to working with other agencies such as the Police, National Criminal Intelligence Service and the National Crime Squad to:
■ Reduce the supply of illegal drugs;
■ Dismantle the criminal gangs that traffic drugs;
■ Help our colleagues around the world tackle illegal drug production and distribution;
■ Deprive traffickers of their assets and proceeds of crime
■ Reduce the harm caused by drugs in the community.

Drug culture

Misuse of Drugs Act 1971 classifies dangerous or otherwise harmful drugs as 'controlled' substances, which means it is illegal to import or export them, possess them, possess them with an intention to supply them to others, or actually supply them without a licence.

These drugs are split into three categories – Class A, B and C – according to the threat they pose to a person's health and to society as a whole:

Class A drugs include those that are widely abused, such as heroin, cocaine, ecstasy, LSD and magic mushrooms.

Class B drugs include amphetamine and speed.

Class C drugs include cannabis, GHB, anabolic steroids and tranquillisers.

Drugs that do the most harm, such as heroin and cocaine, are the priority of the Government's national drugs strategy.

Overseas threat

Illegal manufacture of heroin and cocaine is almost unheard of in the UK.

Most of the drugs taken by British users come from thousands of miles away on different continents. They are shipped into our country by well-organised chains of international criminals. For instance, much of the heroin sold in the UK comes from opium poppies grown in Afghanistan.

It is processed and moved through 'Route Countries' such as Turkey, Iran, Pakistan and the Far East before being smuggled into Britain through Europe.

Cocaine is similar but its origins are more likely to be South American. A great deal is routed through the Caribbean and Mexico, then travels through Spain, Portugal, France, Belgium and the Netherlands before making it into the hands of British dealers.

Belgium and the Netherlands are prime sources of synthetic drugs, such as ecstasy and amphetamine; although production of synthetic drugs appears to be on the rise in the UK, too.

The main source countries for cannabis are Morocco, Russia, Pakistan, Lebanon, Colombia, Mexico, Jamaica and Nigeria.

Smugglers and their techniques

Traffickers try a huge variety of scams to get past Customs officers. We routinely seize drugs that have been:

- Swallowed or stuffed by someone into their body cavity;
- Hidden on a person;
- Packed into someone's luggage or belongings;
- Stashed in a car, boat or aeroplane;
- Hidden in seemingly legitimate freight.

The effective control of drugs was introduced through legislation such as the Misuse of Drugs Act 1971 which classified dangerous or otherwise harmful drugs to be controlled. Centuries of experience in dealing with smugglers have taught us where some of the biggest risks are and what to look out for.

> *Most of the drugs taken by British users come from thousands of miles away on different continents*

Our officers develop detailed intelligence, which helps us target attempted smuggling of drugs that follow unusual sea or air routes – yachts that throw huge bundles of drugs overboard in secluded coves, for instance.

Examples of Customs drug seizures for 2002/03 include:

- **Heroin** 2,070 kilogrammes
- **Cocaine** 8,767 kilogrammes
- **Ecstasy** 668 kilogrammes
- **Cannabis** 59,034 kilogrammes

Number of people sentenced for drug offences: 1,359.

Average length of sentence: 63 months or approx. 5 years.

A vital source of help is information from the public to our Customs Confidential Hotline or through C&E close links to trade organisations.

The use of guns and violence

Some drugs gangs use the threat of extreme violence to protect their lucrative cargo. It's not just detection which threatens their shipments, but theft by rival criminals.

A kilo of heroin costs less than £1,000 in Pakistan but on British streets it is worth more than 75 times as much.

This potential profit has drawn major organised crime syndicates to drug smuggling – the Mafia and Jamaican Yardies are known to be involved.

But trafficking also carries massive risks, including some of the most severe international legal penalties.

This means that some drug traffickers are violent and carry guns. It means our officers – who are unarmed – have to work closely with armed police specialists to stop these potentially ruthless criminals.

International co-operation has led to a significant reduction in the number of drug swallowers detected entering the UK. In the year before the UK-Jamaica partnership to deter cocaine-swallowing smuggling – Operation Airbridge – the number of cocaine swallowers detected in the UK had risen rapidly to 730.

With the deterrent effect produced by the operation, this number fell dramatically to 185 in the operation's first year up to June 2003, and in the last year up to June 2004, the number has been reduced further to only 41 – a total reduction of more than 90 per cent since the operation began.

Our officers

Tackling Class A drug smuggling is one of Customs' top priorities. We have

units of specialist investigators and dedicated anti-smuggling teams at ports and airports that can deal with any situation quickly and professionally and at a moment's notice 24 hours a day.

But it isn't just on land we operate. Customs and Excise's four ships called cutters guard Britain's coastline. Nor is it just humans involved in the anti-trafficking effort. Detector dogs have recorded enormous successes throughout their decades of service.

The most severe penalties

People who are caught smuggling drugs can be fined a lot of money and sent to prison for a long time.

- Class A – Supply and/or dealing: up to 25 years (life) in prison, an unlimited fine or both.
  Possession: up to 7 years imprisonment, an unlimited fine or both.

Class A drugs include those that are widely abused, such as heroin, cocaine, ecstasy, LSD and magic mushrooms

---

- Class B – Supply and/or dealing: up to 14 years in prison, an unlimited fine or both.
  Possession: up to 5 years' imprisonment, an unlimited fine or both.
- Class C – Supply and/or dealing: up to 14 years in prison, an unlimited fine or both.
  Possession: up to 2 years' imprisonment, an unlimited fine or both.

Our powers also allow us to confiscate the criminal's money and possessions if they are the proceeds of their crimes. We are also able to seize any money that we find being moved in or out of the country if we can prove that it is being used for drug smuggling.

- The above information is reprinted with kind permission from HM Revenue and Customs. For more information please visit their website at www.hmrc.gov.uk

© *Crown copyright*

New laws for magic mushrooms

Information from FRANK

The new Drugs Act 2005 has changed the law so that now both fresh and prepared (e.g. dried or stewed) magic mushrooms are classified as Class A drugs. Possession can get you up to seven years in jail and an unlimited fine. Supplying someone else with magic mushrooms can get you life and an unlimited fine.

How has the law changed?

The law has changed so that fresh mushrooms containing psilocin or psilocybin, as well as the chemicals themselves, are classified as Class A drugs. Previously only prepared (e.g. dried or stewed) magic mushrooms were in this category. The reason for the new laws is to stop the commercial sale of hallucinogenic mushrooms. It is now an offence to import, export, produce, supply or possess with intent to supply magic mushrooms, including the raw psilocybe mushrooms. The law also now covers production so it is illegal to supply growing kits.

Why are psilocin and psilocybin Class A?

Psilocin and psilocybin are powerful hallucinogenics like LSD – in other words, they give you a trip. These trips can be a good or bad experience – if bad they can leave you disorientated, paranoid, frightened and sick, and you may experience flashbacks. Magic mushrooms are particularly harmful to people with mental illness or with an underlying mental health problem.

What if you have magic mushrooms growing naturally in your garden?

The Government has brought in regulations to make clear under what circumstances it will not be against the law to possess magic mushrooms. Exceptions will be made for people who unknowingly pick the mushrooms in the wild or find them growing in their garden.

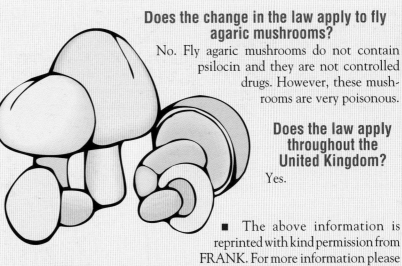

Does the change in the law apply to fly agaric mushrooms?

No. Fly agaric mushrooms do not contain psilocin and they are not controlled drugs. However, these mushrooms are very poisonous.

Does the law apply throughout the United Kingdom?

Yes.

- The above information is reprinted with kind permission from FRANK. For more information please visit www.talktofrank.com or if you wish to write to them, please see page 41 for their contact details.

© *Crown copyright*

35

Busted!

What will happen if you are arrested

If you get arrested …
- Be polite. If you are rude or angry, it won't hurt the police a bit but it might affect how they treat you. Being polite may get you home faster.
- Call an adult. It is the law that if you are under 17, the police cannot officially interview you or caution you without 'an appropriate adult' being there – like your parents, guardians, social worker or even a teacher you know well. If that adult is not there, any evidence you give doesn't count.
- You don't have to say anything or sign anything till the adult turns up. It is also your right to call the duty solicitor who will make sure you are treated fairly.

Excuses which don't work
'They're for a friend.' This counts as supplying drugs and makes things worse. Even if you were just handing some round free, it's still supply.

'They're not mine, I'm just keeping them for a friend.' If you know you have drugs on you, it's illegal.

What the police will do
If the police think you have committed a drug offence, they use the Case Disposal System to choose what to do with you. This gives them four choices:
- Proceed to prosecution.
- Give a formal caution.
- Give a formal warning.
- Not to proceed.

Each case is decided on its own merits. The following information is taken from the police's own guide on how to deal with drug offenders.

Proceed to prosecution
This means going to court. In young people's crime, they try to avoid this for your sake. However, if you have been caught supplying drugs (selling or giving them) or trafficking (carrying large quantities for yourself or for someone else), the police will come down much harder on you. Under the terms of the Misuse of Drugs Act (1971), the punishments for Class A drugs, like heroin, cocaine, crack, LSD and ecstasy are:
- Possession: from 6 months' jail plus £5,000 fine, up to 7 years and unlimited fine.
- Supply/trafficking: from six months' jail plus £5,000 fine, up to life and unlimited fine.

Even if you were just handing some drugs round free, it's still supply

---

The punishments for Class B drugs like cannabis, speed and other amphetamines (unless injected) are:
- Possession: from 3 months plus £500 fine up to 5 years and unlimited fine.
- Supply/trafficking: 6 months plus £5,000 fine up to 14 years and unlimited fine.

For Class C drugs, like mild sedatives, painkillers, and sleeping pills, the penalties are:
- Possession: from 3 months plus £500 fine, up to 2 years plus unlimited fine.
- Supply/trafficking: 3 months plus £5,000 fine, up to 5 years plus unlimited fine.

In other words, massive penalties. It just isn't worth the risk.

Formal caution
Formal cautions are used to deal quickly and simply with less serious offenders. It stops you going to court, but it means you won't want to do it again. It means you get a criminal record held on the national police database. This could wreck your chances of getting a job, or a visa to go on holiday. If you get caught again, your caution can be counted against you in court making the sentence worse. In any case, you are more likely to be prosecuted if you get caught again.

The police give a caution when:
- they have enough evidence to make a successful prosecution, but want to keep you out of the courts, jail etc.
- they are sure your parents or guardian understand how serious it is and agree that you ought to be cautioned.

Formal warning
Formal warnings are less serious than cautions, and are given for minor offences – generally if you're caught with Class B or C drugs (cannabis, speed) for your own use. You don't get a criminal record, but:
- a record will be kept for three years of your name and offence at the local station
- a previous warning may influence the decision whether or not to prosecute if you offend again.

Sounds a bit tame? You guessed it, there's a catch. If you have been caught with ecstasy or any other Class A drug, it counts as too serious an offence to get just a formal warning. The police guide says they must caution or prosecute you and you'll get the criminal record. And the same goes if you have been selling drugs to anyone else, even just cannabis. And of course, if they get arrested then the police will be asking who the drugs came from…

Not proceeded with
This means that the police have enough evidence you're guilty, but having considered the circumstances, they decide not to do anything further. Any offence can be treated this way.

- The above information is reprinted with kind permission from Doctor Ann. For more information please visit www.doctorann.org

© *Teenage Health Websites Ltd*

Cannabis: a question of classification

Information from FRANK

You may have heard rumours that the government is thinking about reversing its decision to reclassify cannabis from Class B to Class C and move it back to Class B. What's going on?

Here are answers to some of the questions you've been asking. For other information about cannabis, contact FRANK.

Last year cannabis was moved from Class B to Class C because it was considered to be less harmful than other Class B drugs such as speed

Has the government changed its mind about cannabis?

No. The government has asked for a review of cannabis and its association with mental health problems and advice on claims of more usage of increased strength cannabis, which will be done by the Advisory Council on the Misuse of Drugs (ACMD). They will report back with recommendations later this year (2005), we cannot predict what the ACMD will recommend. In the meantime, nothing changes – cannabis continues to be an illegal Class C drug.

What's the difference between a Class B drug and a Class C drug?

The law puts illegal drugs into three classes: A, B and C – according to the harm that they can do to you and your communities. Class A is the most harmful. Last year cannabis was moved from Class B to Class C

FRANK

0800 77 66 00   talktofrank.com
Friendly, confidential drugs advice

because it was considered to be less harmful than other Class B drugs such as speed.

Is it likely that cannabis will go back to Class B?

We will have to wait and see as the Advisory Council on the Misuse of Drugs (ACMD) will be making its recommendations to the government later this year. Then it's up to the government to decide whether cannabis will stay as a Class C drug.

The ACMD has not been asked for advice on reclassifying cannabis back to Class B. It has been asked to look at two health-related issues that the government is concerned about:

1. The link between cannabis and mental health problems. Although it is not clear if cannabis can actually cause mental illness, it can make things worse for

people who already have mental health problems. Anyone with mental health problems or people who are most at risk of getting them (e.g. have a family history of schizophrenia) should avoid cannabis. The ACMD will review the latest medical research in this area.

2. The availability of stronger cannabis, such as skunk. The chemical in cannabis that makes you feel high is called THC. Cannabis comes in a variety of different strengths depending on the amount of THC in it – the more THC, the stronger it is. Some people claim that stronger cannabis is now more available than before, and the ACMD will look into this.

When will the ACMD finish their review?

The review should be finished by around December 2005. Check out www.talktofank.com for the latest.

■ The above information is reprinted with kind permission from FRANK. Visit www.talktofrank.com or see page 41 for contact details.

© *Crown copyright*

Cannabis and mental health

Heavy use of cannabis may lead to psychotic symptoms in susceptible individuals

New research appearing in the journal *Addiction* supports the growing evidence that cannabis can seriously damage mental health.

Cannabis is thought by many to be a harmless recreational drug and is used regularly by people of all ages although research over many years has shown that people who use cannabis regularly are more likely to suffer from schizophrenia. What has not been clear is whether the symptoms are caused by cannabis use or whether people who are likely to develop psychotic symptoms happen also to be more likely to be attracted to cannabis.

Cannabis is thought by many to be a harmless recreational drug and is used regularly by people of all ages

---

In the *Addiction* paper, Professor David Fergusson and colleagues from the Christchurch School of Medicine and Health Sciences, University of Otago, in New Zealand, used data gathered across the course of a 25-year study of over 1,000 New Zealanders born in 1977. They devised complex statistical models that took into account the possibility that psychosis encouraged cannabis use, and that also adjusted the results for other factors associated with cannabis use. The fact that this was a prospective study allowed the researchers to get a better understanding of the direction of effect. Said David Fergusson, 'Even when all factors were taken into account, there was a clear increase in rates of psychotic symptoms after the start of regular use, with daily users of cannabis having rates that were over 150% those of non-users. These findings add to a growing body of evidence from different sources,

all of which suggest that heavy use of cannabis may lead to increased risks of psychotic symptoms and illness in susceptible individuals.'
1 March 2005

- The above information is reprinted with kind permission from *Addiction*. For more information visit www.addictionjournal.org

© *Addiction*

Cannabis: the facts

The facts

- Cannabis is the most commonly used illicit drug. Around three million adults have used cannabis in the last year.
- 11% of 16- to 59-year-olds and 26.2% of 16- to 24-year-olds have used cannabis in the last year.
- Cannabis use has become increasingly widespread in the UK since the 1960s.
- Cannabis has been used by over half (55 per cent) of young men and over a third (44 per cent) of young women aged 16 to 29 years.

What is cannabis?

Cannabis is derived from a family of bushes (*cannabis sativa, ruderalis, indica* and *gigantea*), which contain varying degrees of psychoactive compounds.

The hemp fibre from these plants has been used for millennia in the manufacture of all sorts of products such as rope, mats, clothing, paints and varnishes. The plants have also been used for a pleasurable effect and for medicinal and ritual purposes. The leaves and flowers, which can either be processed into resin or oil or dried, are then smoked, made into herbal tea or eaten.

What is in cannabis?

The main psychoactive ingredient in cannabis is tetrahydrocannabinol (THC).

Some experts have claimed that the cannabis available now is far stronger than that used in the 1960s, but this is difficult to substantiate. The supply of more potent cannabis products in recent years may have been encouraged by the success of law enforcement in detecting and destroying large-scale cannabis plantations, creating an incentive for illicit suppliers of cannabis to grow small numbers of cannabis plants with a higher THC content (e.g. hydroponic cultivation). Many people in the UK have decided to cultivate their own cannabis to ensure good quality.

The law

The government reclassified cannabis from a Class B to a Class C drug in January 2004.

If caught in possession of cannabis, those 17 or under can be arrested and taken to a police station for a formal warning. If it is not a first offence it could result in a conviction.

Those over 18 can have their drugs confiscated and receive a warning. Police can still arrest an individual if they are a repeat offender, are smoking in public, are a threat to public order or have cannabis near any premises used by children. The maximum penalty for supplying and dealing Class C drugs is still 14 years plus an unlimited fine.

© *Action on Addiction*

Should drugs be legalised?

Information from DrugScope

The call for the present drug laws to be changed has come from many quarters. The reasons for wanting change and for maintaining them are given here. The debate itself can be broken down into three key elements:

- Civil liberties versus the duty of the state;
- The harm caused by drugs and enforcing prohibition;
- How would a legalised regime be managed?

Civil liberties

Freedom to use

The degree to which the state is justified in interfering in the private life of the citizen thereby restricting freedom of choice is hotly debated. The principle of personal choice is applied to a wide range of private activities and why not drug use?

Duty to protect

On the other hand, if, by using drugs, an individual is causing significant harm to themselves or others, the state can rightfully seek to counteract that harm. Compulsory wearing of seatbelts is an example. In legislating against drug use, the government is seen to be discouraging a potentially harmful behaviour. Legalising any drug would be sending out the message to society that intoxication is a sanctioned behaviour.

Harm

Health impact

Increasingly health is cited as the main reason for prohibition. The latest international review of cannabis by the World Health Organisation highlights dangers such as lung and throat cancer, and increasing incidence of mental health problems due to prolonged heavy use in a minority of users. Consideration should also be given to whether the harm drugs cause, which may not be great for many users, warrants the government's intervention.

The harm of current laws

While the drug laws are there to prevent what the government sees as harmful behaviour, some see them as harmful in themselves. They are seen as making users criminals, creating strong and lucrative black markets and stigmatising those who need help the most – the addicts.

> *The degree to which the state is justified in interfering in the private life of the citizen thereby restricting freedom of choice is hotly debated*

How would legalisation be managed?

Crucial to the debate on legalisation are the issues around the practicalities of one situation over another. On the one hand making drugs legal and more available will result in more use and so increase the incidence of harmful side effects – at great cost to society. On the other hand, removing a black market could raise drug-related revenues to the government, save on police costs and help regulate the sale and consumption of drugs through regulated sales (as is done with alcohol).

One drug leads to another – escalation theory

Cannabis and other drugs are often regarded as providing a 'gateway' to more or problematic drug use. This is known as escalation theory.

All that can be said is that most people who use heroin will have previously used cannabis (though only a small proportion of those who try cannabis go on to use heroin). This could be because cannabis actually does (at least for some people) lead to heroin use, but there are alternative explanations. People tend to use cannabis first simply because they come across it first.

Therapeutic use

Another dimension to the reform debate has been the use of cannabis for therapeutic purposes. The British Medical Association has lent its support to calls for further research and GW Pharmaceuticals, which specialises in developing clinical drugs from cannabis, has completed clinical trials of its spray-administered Sativex drug.

- Information from DrugScope. Visit www.drugscope.org.uk for more.
  © *DrugScope*

KEY FACTS

■ A drug is any substance, solid, liquid or gas that brings about physical and/or psychological changes in the body. (page 1)

■ There are three main types of drugs, classified according to the effect the drug has on the central nervous system: depressants, stimulants and hallucinogens. (page 1)

■ A regular heroin user (using monthly or more often) will spend on average £447.40 per month on their habit. (page 2)

■ In 2003, 33 deaths from drug poisoning by amphetamines (speed) were recorded. (page 3)

■ Humans may have an evolutionary predisposition to seek out narcotics, even though they can be addictive and damaging. Some people may have genes which make them more genetically prone to drug addiction. (page 4)

■ Individual ecstasy pills can now be bought for as little as 50p in Portsmouth and 80p in Cardiff. (page 6)

■ Heavy ecstasy users are at risk of long-term mental impairment, according to a study published in the international journal *Addiction*. (page 8)

■ Almost 9 per cent of under-25s now admit having taken cocaine. (page 9)

■ Crack use is rising with 79,000 people admitting to using the drug in the last year compared to 63,000 in previous years. This means that more people now admit to using crack than to using heroin (64,000). (page 10)

■ All drugs have an adverse impact; but heroin and crack are by far the most addictive, expensive and harmful drugs. (page 12)

■ Figures published by the Office for National Statistics for 1999 to 2003 show that drug-related deaths fell for the third year in a row to reach their lowest level since 1997. (page 13)

■ If current trends continue the numbers addicted to class A drugs could reach the one million mark by 2025. (page 14)

■ Addiction means a person has no control over whether he or she uses a drug. A person who's addicted has grown so used to a drug that he or she has to have it. Addiction can be physical, psychological, or both. (page 17)

■ More than a quarter of those aged 14 and 15 have tried cannabis. (page 20)

■ In 2004, 10% of pupils had taken drugs in the last month. 18% of pupils had taken drugs in the last year. (page 21)

■ More than one in seven (14%) young drivers aged 17-25 admit putting lives at risk by driving after taking illegal drugs. (page 23)

■ Volatile substance abuse (VSA) is responsible for more deaths among children aged 10 to 16 in the UK than illegal drugs. (page 27)

■ Although it is not illegal to sniff solvents, it is illegal to sell them to young people. The Intoxicating Substances Supply Act (1985) made it an offence to supply someone under the age of 18 yrs with a substance known to 'achieve intoxication'. (page 27)

■ Volatile substances include hairspray, glue, nail varnish remover, deodorant, various aerosols and solvents. At 15% of all 15 to 16-year-olds the UK has the highest level of solvent use in the EU. (page 28)

■ In a survey by Student Direct, 75% of respondents had ever taken an illegal drug. Excluding cannabis, the figure who had taken illegal drugs was 47%. 50% of these were classified as regular (at least monthly) users. (page 30)

■ Experts estimate the worldwide illegal drugs trade is worth as much as the individual oil, gas or world tourism industries. Whatever the true figure, the UK alone spends more than one billion pounds tackling the problem. (page 33)

■ The new Drugs Act 2005 has changed the law so that now both fresh and prepared (e.g. dried or stewed) magic mushrooms are classified as Class A drugs. (page 35)

■ Cannabis is thought by many to be a harmless recreational drug and is used regularly by people of all ages although research over many years has shown that people who use cannabis regularly are more likely to suffer from schizophrenia. (page 38)

■ Cannabis is the most commonly used illicit drug. Around three million adults have used cannabis in the last year. 11% of 16- to 59-year-olds and 26.2% of 16- to 24-year-olds have used cannabis in the last year. (page 38)

■ Increasingly health is cited as the main reason for drug prohibition. The latest international review of cannabis by the World Health Organization highlights dangers such as lung and throat cancer, and increasing incidence of mental health problems due to prolonged heavy use in a minority of users. (page 39)

ADDITIONAL RESOURCES

You might like to contact the following organisations for further information. Due to the increasing cost of postage, many organisations cannot respond to enquiries unless they receive a stamped, addressed envelope.

Action on Addiction
1st Floor, Park Place
12 Lawn Lane
LONDON SW8 1UD
Tel: 020 7793 1011
Fax: 020 7793 8549
Email: action@aona.co.uk
Website: www.aona.co.uk

Australian Drug Foundation
409 King Street
West Melbourne VIC 3051
AUSTRALIA
Tel: +61 3 9278 8138
Fax: +61 3 9328 3008
Email: druginfo@adf.org.au
Website: www.adf.org.au

Barnardo's
Tanners Lane
Barkingside
ILFORD
Essex IG6 1QG
Tel: 020 8550 8822
Fax: 020 8551 6870
Email:
dorothy.howes@barnardos.org.uk
Website: www.barnardos.org.uk
Barnardo's works with over 47,000
children, young people and their
families in more than 300 projects
across the country. This includes
work with children affected by
today's most urgent issues:
homelessness, poverty, disability,
bereavement and abuse.

Brake
PO Box 548
HUDDERSFIELD
Yorkshire HD1 2XZ
Tel: 01484 559909
Fax: 01484 559983
Email: brake@brake.org.uk
Website: www.brake.org.uk
Brake is a national road safety
charity with two aims:
- To prevent death and injury on
  the roads through education of
  all road users and campaigning
  for Government improvements
  to road safety.
- To care for people who are
  bereaved or affected by serious

injury in a road crash through
support services, including a
helpline and literature
distributed through police
officers.

British Psychological Society
St Andrews House
48 Princess Road East
LEICESTER LE1 7DR
Tel: 0116 2549568
Fax: 0116 2470787
Email: enquiries@bps.org.uk
Website: www.bps.org.uk
Advances the education and
practice of psychologists.

Doctor Ann's Virtual Surgery
19 Beaumont Street
OXFORD OX1 2NA
Tel: 01865 240501
Email: ann.mcpherson@gp-
k84016.nhs.uk
Websites: www.doctorann.org
www.teenagehealthfreak.org
Teenage Health Websites Limited
is the brainchild of Drs Ann Mc-
Pherson and Aidan Macfarlane,
writers of the original Diary of a
Teenage Health Freak series. The
worldwide success of the diaries
identified a demand for cringe-free
health information specific to
teenagers. The books sold over half
a million copies in the UK and
have been translated into 22
languages.

DrugScope
Waterbridge House
32-36 Loman Street
LONDON SE1 0EE
Tel: 020 7928 1211
Fax: 020 7928 1771
Email: info@drugscope.org.uk
Website: www.drugscope.org.uk
DrugScope is the UK's leading
independent centre of expertise on
drugs. Our aim is to inform policy
development and reduce drug-
related risk. We provide quality
drug information, promote
effective responses to drug taking,
undertake research at local,

national and international levels,
advise on policy-making,
encourage informed debate and
speak for our member organisations working on the ground.

FRANK Campaign
Tel: 020 7544 3111
Emails:
FRANK@homeoffice.gsi.gov.uk
frank@talktofrank.com
Website: www.talktofrank.com
FRANK is an 'umbrella' brand
which can join up all drugs
communications. FRANK was
launched in May 2003 and since
then there have been over 4
million visits to its drug
information website
talktofrank.com and 700,000 calls
to its helpline – 0800 77 66 00.
The campaign targets 11- to 21-
year-olds, and the parents of 11- to
18-year-olds, but the service is for
everyone and FRANK can be used
and adapted locally for your own
drug campaign needs.

*National Children's Bureau
(NCB)*
8 Wakley Street
LONDON EC1V 7QE
Tel: 020 7843 6000
Fax: 020 7843 9512
Email: koshea@ncb.org.uk
Website: www.ncb.org.uk
The National Children's Bureau
(NCB) promotes the interests and
well-being of all children and
young people across every aspect of
their lives. We advocate the
participation of children and
young people in all matters
affecting them.

*United Nations Office on Drugs
and Crime*
Vienna International Centre
PO Box 500
A-1400 Vienna
AUSTRIA
Tel: 00 43 1 26060 0
Fax: 00 43 1 26060 5866
Website: www.unodc.org

INDEX

ACKNOWLEDGEMENTS

The publisher is grateful for permission to reproduce the following material.

While every care has been taken to trace and acknowledge copyright, the publisher tenders its apology for any accidental infringement or where copyright has proved untraceable. The publisher would be pleased to come to a suitable arrangement in any such case with the rightful owner.

Chapter One: Drug Misuse

About drugs, © Australian Drug Foundation, *Instant expert*, © New Scientist, *Seven important drugs terms*, © Crown copyright is reproduced with the permission of Her Majesty's Stationery Office, *Trading places*, © DrugScope, *Ketamine*, © Crown copyright is reproduced with the permission of Her Majesty's Stationery Office, *Ecstasy could harm memory*, © Blackwells, *Ecstasy*, © Teenage Health Websites Limited, *The cocaine explosion*, © 2005 Associated Newspapers Ltd, *Tackling crack misuse*, © DrugScope, *Cocaine/crack*, © Teenage Health Websites Limited, *Revealed: how drugs war failed*, © Guardian Newspapers Ltd 2005, *Understanding the issues*, © Crown copyright is reproduced with the permission of Her Majesty's Stationery Office, *Drug-related deaths down for the third year running*, © Crown copyright is reproduced with the permission of Her Majesty's Stationery Office, *Drug user numbers set to treble*, © Guardian Newspapers Ltd 2005, *World drug use*, © UNODC, *It's all in the mix*, © Crown copyright is reproduced with the permission of Her Majesty's Stationery Office, *Dealing with addiction*, © 1995-2005. The Nemours Foundation, *Know the signs of drug taking*, © Metropolitan Police.

Chapter Two: Drugs and Young People

Quarter of 15-year-olds have tried cannabis, © Telegraph Group Ltd 2005, *The facts*, © Barnardo's, *Drug use and the young*, © NCSR/NFER, *Cheap as chocolate*, © 2005 Associated Newspapers Ltd, *One in seven young drivers drive on drugs*, © Brake, *Young drug users feel neglected by parents*, © British Psychological Society, *Drugs and the family*, © Joseph Rowntree Foundation, *Random drug tests for pupils at start of new school term*, © Telegraph Group Ltd 2005, *Dangerous highs*, © NCB, *Solvents*, © Teenage Health Websites Limited, *In their words*, © Barnardo's, *The score*, © Crown copyright is reproduced with the permission of Her Majesty's Stationery Office.

Chapter Three: Drugs and the Law

The Misuse of Drugs Act 1971, © DrugScope, *Bad deal*, © Crown copyright is reproduced with the permission of Her Majesty's Stationery Office, *Drug smuggling*, © Crown copyright is reproduced with the permission of Her Majesty's Stationery Office, *New laws for magic mushrooms*, © Crown copyright is reproduced with the permission of Her Majesty's Stationery Office, *Busted!*, © Teenage Health Websites Limited, *Cannabis: a question of classification*, © Crown copyright is reproduced with the permission of Her Majesty's Stationery Office, *Cannabis and mental health*, © Addiction, *Cannabis: the facts*, © Action on Addiction, *Should drugs be legalised?*, © DrugScope.

Photographs and illustrations:

Pages 1, 13, 37: Angelo Madrid; pages 4, 29: Pumpkin House; pages 8, 11, 26, 39: Don Hatcher; pages 9, 14, 23, 34: Simon Kneebone; pages 17, 27: Bev Aisbett.

Craig Donnellan
Cambridge
January, 2006